Christian Ministry Organization

[[And I thank Christ Jesus our Lord, who hath enabled me, for that he counted me faithful, putting me into the ministry; 1Tim 1:12]]

Perfection Handbook Series:

Charles P.K. WATCHER

Except otherwise indicated, all bible quotations in this document come from *Free Holy Bible* *The Free Bible* "This Free Bible Program" Developed By Edward Morales; version was created on July 2007

This book is a production of PERFECTION MINISTRY Intl (PMI)

Matt 5:48 Be ye therefore perfect, even as your Father which is in heaven is perfect.

FOREWORD

This book targets the unrepresented question of organizational imperfection in the church. It is a follow-up from another series; the Natural, Horizontal and Vertical gospel prescriptions which direct our appreciation of authentic Christian ministry. In that book, we were taught about ministry gifts and how they are explained within the church. We study here areas of perfecting ministry organization.

Our objective is to teach the different offices that are ordained by God (with entitlements in the gospel). How ministry offices relate to one another and the entire whole. We inspire vision bearers to expand their horizon of interventions with a holistic ministry approach involving all Christian denominations and not only their local assemblies.

Children of God have the opportunity to find their respective callings. Future visioneers meet with the open challenge to use this approach to build their churches. It becomes important that they do not insist to split from parent or mentoring churches especially if God has not sent them with another message.

Only a difference in revelation can split people spiritually. There is absolutely no need to keep splitting churches unless such is as a result of something different and new. Apart from the prayer of our lord Jesus in **John17:11** for unity of believers, the bible as well discourages "church splitting" in **Hebrews 6:1-2**.

No splits on account of dogma. Only split by reason of love **(Col 3:14)**. People may even be united in churches but are actually worlds apart. If ministers adopt the elements of perfection, the rest will follow. This is the will of God for the end time believers **(1Cor 13:10)**.

The organizational set up of the church as represented in the bible is the best possible way of upholding the people of God. No need for hidden or unnecessary offices, positions or dispositions. No need to move to the top by carnal means. Only a spiritual action provokes a "spiritual blessing" and increase.

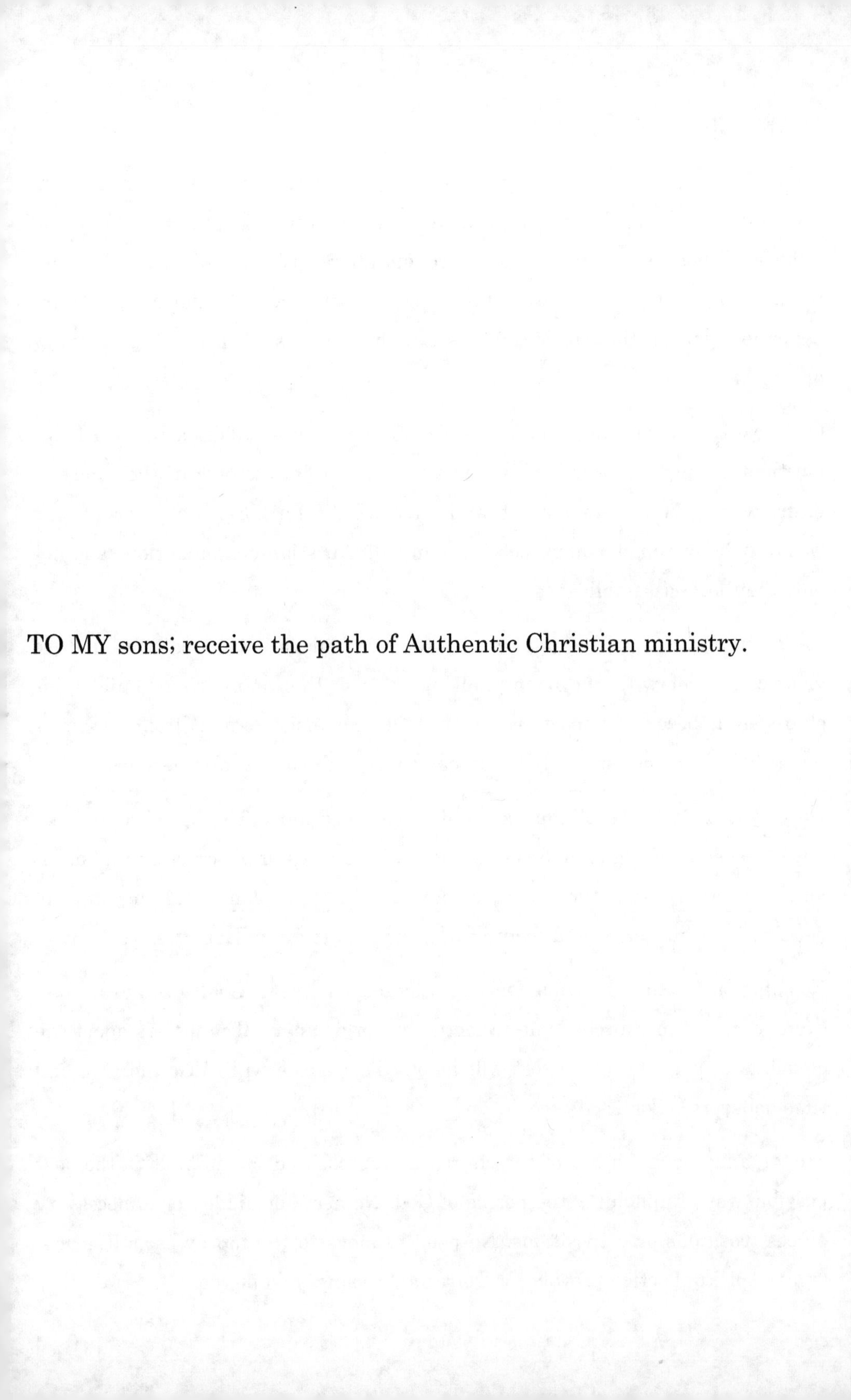

TO MY sons; receive the path of Authentic Christian ministry.

We are already fully successful in the earth being « born again ». We can only make increase. This book will help Christians to flourish in another dimension of biblical knowledge on the Christian mission. This will prompt them to integrate any Christian milieu with ease. To have a positive composure, knowing they are doing the right thing once and for all.

I strongly caution against "institutionalized Christian churches". People cannot and should not come together and vote to start and run a Christian church. God always and still talks today to individuals who then take responsibility for any message received to propagate and to sustain it. They then move in the direction of the revelation as communicated by the Holy Spirit.

You will learn in-between for example that there are no such particular callings in ministry as priests although these words are found all over in the bible. Everyone is called to the priesthood after sanctification. Again, when you read the biblical signification of a bishop, you will understand that there could be no such missionary title as archbishop. The title attributed to conventional bishops also signifying the position of a learning "head pupil" in the bible, could not be expected to command the respect it has today. These and many other common errors ensue because their foundation is not based on scripture but rather a conspiracy to politicize the church of our God.

The lord is bringing his church to an organizational perfection. Position yourselves and every local church to participate effectively in the ministry of Jesus Christ the lord through knowledge. He calls individuals one at a time into ministry (1Tim1:12). The most solicited reader should have gone through the book "Natural, vertical and horizontal gospels". This will help him/her to understand and move along with the project of the perfecting organization for Christian ministry.

The updated structures put in place by the Holy Spirit herein particularly ensures that there is an effective correspondence between Christian churches. This is essential for the end time church. This book is to be used by all vision bearers of Christian ministries to establish lasting impact to the work of God in their mission and field. Any Christian division is of the devil.

The lord wants all his children brought into oneness under one lord and shepherd Jesus Christ. This organizational structuring enables a collaborative organigram for linkages with all the Christian churches. The only reason the bible says Jesus was angry for and whipped many out of his (our) father's house is glaring to our faces. Imperfection has eaten into the fabrics of the Christian church. Money quests and finely polished businesses thrive easily and freely therein. The main reason for division by doctrines **(Heb6:1)**.

I encourage church leaders to work with the perfection organization plan. This plan allows only the Holy Spirit to work wherever he wills. Not in isolated "brainwashing camps" that discriminate and or ignore others. We hence create an environment where children of God stay spiritually alert at all times. Such a place should not essentially promote discrimination and flow of wealth to leaders. This type of Christianity is a new problem on its own right rather than God's solution.

This book is not written for unbelievers nor people who treat the things of God with negligence. Even the many compromising church goers of our day. Those who have no time to search scripture in order to please the father are not themselves followers. It is for sheep and shepherds alike.

To further understand ordination and the dedications associated with this topic, read the book "Symbolic feasts of our perfection". Also contact the perfection ministry website for support and assistance in this or other important projects. It is about God and should be done as God says it.

> *Isaiah 52:7 How beautiful upon the mountains are the feet of him that bringeth good tidings, that publisheth peace; that bringeth good tidings of good, that publisheth salvation; that saith unto Zion, Thy God reigneth!*

This book gives lovers of God the simplest solution and way forward to stop today's unbiblical disorder. The main cause of this whole drama is a misunderstanding of the biblical "Christian Ministry Organization". God wants us to walk orderly **(2Thes 3:11, 1Cor14:40)**. The lord has not done this work to fight individuals but to dismantle a failing system that withal works towards anti-Christian interests **(Luke16:9).** Nobody does God without God.

It is very easy to observe a cultural dance somewhere then go home to start one. However, if you do not understand the pillar beliefs that put up that dance institution, you will be doing a fake or counterfeit version of it.

Dr Charles PK Watcher

ACKNOWLEDGEMENTS

I am indeed grateful to the fathers of the gospel; even the teachers that have with the zeal of hope kept ministering to me and to the saints without ceasing. Without their combined efforts, I may not have embraced this peculiar grace to minister in teaching and with great joy.

I thank specially my father in the lord Pastor Chris Oyakhilome particularly for letting himself be mightily used of the lord in the teaching ministry.

Profound gratitude to the team FREE BIBLE PROGRAM of the free Holy Bible by Edward Morales.

Lastly I thank those whom the lord has strategically used to place me on the right pedestal of spiritual increase both through the fine things and the "unpleasant ones".

NB: While thanking everyone, I recognize and underline that many are still walking amiss sound doctrine, and I believe this book is aimed towards helping them in love.

Table of CONTENTS

Introduction to Christian sanctification

Only for those that choose the narrrow path.

> *[[For this is the will of God, even your sanctification, that every one of you should know how to possess his vessel in sanctification and honour; 1Thes 4:3-4]]*

You cannot be a good minister of the gospel without understanding sanctification. Sanctification is a continuous happening within believers. The lord is keen to see our sanctification and continuous sanctification (**1Thes4:3-4**). The cleaner we get by the word of God, the more sanctified we have become (John 15:3). Many Christians still do not understand that in the spiritual realm, we are in contact directly with the lord by the continual acquisition of truth.

> *Heb 2:11 For both he that sanctifieth and they who are sanctified are all of one: for which cause he is not ashamed to call them brethren,*

The first line of sanctification is salvation. When someone believes and receives the life of God. This is what is termed "being born again". Thereafter, there are two other possible transformative changes that await children of God.

The decision to honour the kingdom of God by sharing the love of God as communicated in Christ Jesus is the important factor that causes this new change. It is the same love we recieved that is transmitted to others. In preaching the gospel, you have made evidence of valuing your own salvation.

Luke 5:32 I came not to call the righteous, but sinners to repentance.

We know that people can be sanctified into the priesthood as were the children of Aaron and also unto the high priesthood as was Aaron himself **(Heb 5:4)**. It is about receiving the word and walking in the light of it. The more sanctified we become, the more we activate the God function inside of us. As such, the more organized the church is with all specialized gifts and the more adapted it becomes to retain truth and to give love.

The important thing about understanding organizational perfection is to situate and to receive the kind of teaching that will enable growth in all spiritual things. The ground on which the teaching of truth is done must be able to hold it. If you do not place people correctly in the house of God, many of them will function presumptuously; hazardously destroying what is being built by others.

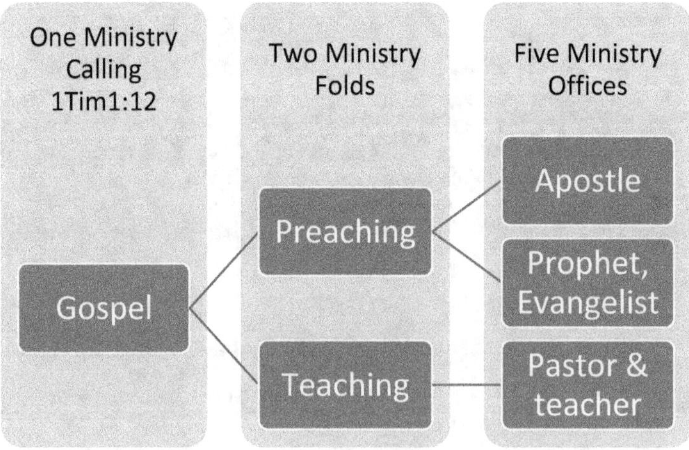

*Figure 1 Eph4:11: And he gave some, apostles; and some, prophets; and some, evangelists; and **some,** pastors and teachers;*

Let no man of God become anscious to call himself a teacher. It is not given to men by their idea of ministry **(Heb 3 5:4)**. I knew that I was called as a teacher not by word of men, the lord himself revealed this to me.

> *2Tim1:11 Whereunto I am appointed a preacher, and an apostle, and a teacher of the Gentiles. 1:12 For the which cause I also suffer these things: nevertheless I am not ashamed: for I know whom I have believed, and am persuaded that he is able to keep that which I have committed unto him against that day. 1:13 Hold fast the form of sound words, which thou hast heard of me, in faith and love which is in Christ Jesus.*

However, Paul could distinguish different functions in his ministry **(2Tim 1:11)** which should galvanize the church of today in similar manner to identify and put all these entitlements to profit the work of God. He maximized his entitlements in the gospel. If I say that I am a teacher, it also means that I am a pastor, an apostle, evangelist and prophet. But dedicated officers cannot say they are pastors or teachers.

Sanctification is an upstream happening **(1Thes 4:3-4)** is a separation from other relationships of the world in order to fully walk with God. While this book focuses to inform the church about the biblical structures that should help to perfect the walk with God in the earth, it is also a reminder to all Christians. They too have an individual choice about their destiny in Christ Jesus.

Walk in sanctification by working out things with the word of God. Either to go ahead to become the best that God wanted you to become as spiritual children or to remain lukewarm and forsake deeper realities of God. When you come to God, your whole self is his sacrifice **(Rom 12:1- 3)**. God takes nothing less from the sanctified.

> *Psalms 50:5 Gather my saints together unto me; those that have made a covenant with me by sacrifice.*

Sanctification is not merely physical, it is inside. You can lie on the same bed with someone and have nothing to do with such **(1Cor5:10)**. Hate their deeds but love them. Not like the Hutterites do, but receiving power from God to be a child of God.

CHAPTER 1: GOD's will in THE Christian CHURCH

Spiritual oneness The God-driven purpose.

[[... that YE BE PERFECTLY JOINED together in the same mind and in the same judgment. 1Cor1:10:])

1.1 GOD'S FAMILY

The Christian family is defined in the book of **Hebrews12:22-24.** It has a spiritual household of God. It has nothing to do with organized institutions and magnificient mega church buildings. Of course, the house of God starts from the hearts of men who love as God does. When a man becomes born again, the bible says you become connected to "the church" of the first born. Not some churches and magnificient buildings in plural.

> *Heb 12:22 But ye are come unto mount Sion, and unto the city of the living God, the heavenly Jerusalem, and to an innumerable company of angels, 12:23 To the general assembly and CHURCH OF THE FIRSTBORN, which are written in heaven, and to God the Judge of all, and to the spirits of just men made perfect, 12:24 And to Jesus the mediator of the new covenant, and to the blood of sprinkling,*

There are privileges in belonging to this wonderful family of God. We live with countless angels for example. We have Jesus the mediator and advocate.

Needless to say that people who multiply churches for private gain are not members of this church. The starting point of every church is in the heart of one man "hearing and doing the word of God and then spreading abroad to other untamed hearts". The church is God's Family, and belongs to the first born of many, Jesus Christ **(Rom 8:29)**.

Without a spiritual oneness, nobody can become like God who is always flourishing inside love; that is inside a relationship. Every believer must be involved in one way or another in promoting unity of believers as desired by the lord **(John 17:11)**. Perfection is only possible in ONE **(John 17:23)**.

1.2 GOD'S FAMILY CRISIS

> *1Cor 1:10 Now I beseech you, brethren, by the name of our Lord Jesus Christ, that ye all speak the same thing, and that there be no divisions among you; but that YE BE PERFECTLY JOINED together in the same mind and in the same judgment.*

It is unfortunate to see that Christian churches keep splitting daily. But this is not the actual problem. The split is not about people going their seperate ways. It is about people receiving diverse pockets of doctrine (revelations). We cannot prevent people disagreeing on small things and even asking God to be their witness in wrong doing but we can take responsibility to teach them the ideal things. God will best have them organized to prevent any future repetitions, the problem will get solved one day.

Even now the prophetic utterance of the end time is a sure petition of unity in perfect things **(1Cor 13:10)**. Christian churches are destined to face important challenges as a result of doctrinal and leadership struggles. This is because even those that are spiritual babies often never want to agree that the issue is not only about age and learning. It is about the power and favour of God at work in individuals according to his will and purposes.

1.3 RESOLVING THIS CRISIS

While we encourage zeal for the things of God, I recommend that

1.3.1 Starting New churches

DO NOT start another church ministry except it is absolutely necessary (there is no counter revelation to the word of God). Notice that if God sends you to start a church; he will provide you with a special message. This message though inspired by God will often be at variance with that received around you. Remember that you are not sent to become an expert critic but rather to bring about new hope and restoration.

1.3.2 Preserve church oneness

Remain strongly connected to your parent ministry or local assembly so that the change taking place around you should influence them positively.

1.3.3 Make connections

Affiliate with other Christian churches. As much as possible, respect and speak well about the work of God's Spirit in the lives of other Christian ministers.

1.3.4 Two important things to note

I) DON'T FIGHT

We should not fight other people and men of God except we are sure God sent us. The sign that God sent any person is that s/he will highlight a problem and also present a solution. The solution and not the problem is the important sign. Starting a church is to reveal something New (teachers) or to build on something that already exists. All servants of God posing as teachers, must have a new message. God doesn't like expert critics, who will see everything wrong about anything except about themselves **(Rom 14:4)**. As long as you do not have a proposal to give to change a declining people or situation that went wrong, the obvious thing is that God has not sent you. Keep quiet and pray while waiting to be sent. Do not follow the manner of the false prophets; do not start a New church for casting and binding demons. God doesn't send people without a message.

Rom 14:4 Who art thou that judgest another man's servant? to his own master he standeth or falleth. Yea, he shall be holden up: for God is able to make him stand. Jesus said it is his word that delivers, heals and restores. A man that has no growing root in the word of God is a wolf.

II) DO YOUR JOB HUMBLY

Luke 10:18 And he said unto them, I beheld Satan as lightning fall from heaven. 10:19 Behold, I give unto you power to tread on serpents and scorpions, and over all the power of the enemy: and nothing shall by any means hurt you. 10:20 Notwithstanding in this rejoice not, that the spirits are subject unto you; but rather rejoice, because your names are written in heaven.

Do not seek to grow because you have a yearn to be famous and celebrated? God's spirit is not like that. Seek to serve him only in a simple and constant simplicity. The Holy Spirit therefore must lead at all times your spiritual ambitions. If your own ambitions fall in-between, fast and pray until you have no such satanic influences before you push on. Do not be derailed from the start. You have a responsibility to decide which spirit you will be subject to.

1.4 PRAYER FOR THE CHURCH

John 17:9 I pray for them: I pray not for the world, but for them which thou hast given me; for they are thine.

Our lord does not pray just for anybody but for the ones that are called by the father. This is why study of the word of God is not facultative. The wisdom of God comes by a directed attention to his word **(Isaiah 66:1-2)**. Nothing ever spoken in this world moved me like in John17. In this scripture, each of us has the opportunity to see the lord, know him, know what he is made of, know that he loves us with an unfathomable passion. We have been invited to the son life and brotherhood of God in Christ Jesus without reserve. Jesus prayed for the unity of Christians all over the world.

John 17:11 And now I am no more in the world, but these are in the world, and I come to thee. Holy Father, keep through thine own name those whom thou hast given me, that they may be one, as we are. 17:23 I in them, and thou in me, that they may be made perfect in one; and that the world may know that thou hast sent me, and hast loved them, as thou hast loved me. 17:24 Father, I will that they also, whom thou hast given me, be with me where I am; that they may behold my glory, which thou hast given me: for thou lovedst me before the foundation of the world.

1.5 ALLOCATING POSITIONS OF RESPONSIBILITY IN THE CHURCH

We will soon study the ministry entitlements and underlying titles. The lord has confided into our hands, specific responsibilities; calling us into the ministry (1Tim1:12). God did not tell Samuel to go and get David. Rather he told Samuel to search for his anointed in the house of Jesse. God does not tell us the name of the called, he shows us the pathway to the called. We have a partial ministry responsibility of faith to select the anointed/chosen from amongst the called.

1Tim 1:12 And I thank Christ Jesus our Lord, who hath enabled me, for that he counted me faithful, putting me into the ministry;

The ministry entitlements represent the things that God has endowed his servants to do from heaven. Titles on the other hand are the functions that men give each other to exert influence on them and to retain privileges. Note first of all our **responsibility to dedicate** them that the lord has given entitlements (apostles, prophets, evangelists, and pastors and teachers). Therefore, we must render the gifts of God available to all in the assembly of God's people.

They are not the same as those we meet on neutral ground. The influence on « the called » is essentially by the Holy Spirit. We can only agree with Him that is master of the harvest. It is also our **duty to ordain** the ones that we meet that are prospective candidates for God's grace of entitlements. We give them the titles and wait until such a time that the grace of God works through them. When they are grown as such by the spirit of God, we proceed to dedicate them to his service.

All that is dedicated belongs to God and his house. That which is ordained receives impartation from that which the lord has already blessed (dedicated). It is the will of the lord Jesus that nobody should come into his family and not receive an introductory title and eventually an entitlement. The final title however comes afterwards for everyone even as it was for Jesus when he finished his ministry.

> NB: Even if anyone comes and says s/he is to be dedicated and not just ordained, there is no problem. Pray and do the dedication. No matter what we do, there are bad fish in the net of preaching. Jesus Christ never stopped doing his ministry because of the presence of a certain Judas Iscariot **(John 6:70)**.

People who tell (smart) lies all the time are ministry Judases. However, let everyone be. Let us love them, teaching in and out of season **(2Tim4:2)**. We now move on to study the entitlements of ministry. Beware of running your ministry with titles **(Matt 19:30)**.

> *Matt 19:28-30And Jesus said unto them, Verily I say unto you, That ye which have followed me, in the regeneration... And every one that hath forsaken houses, or brethren, or sisters, or father, or mother, or wife, or children, or lands, for my name's sake, shall receive an hundredfold, and shall inherit everlasting life. But many that are first shall be last; and the last shall be first.*

CHAPTER 2: Gospel entitlements

Composition of Christian Ministry ...the brain of authentic ministry

[[And he gave some, apostles; and some, prophets; and some, evangelists; and some, pastors and teachers; Eph 4:11]]

2.1 ORGANIZING THE GOSPEL

The words of our lord in **John 15:3** carry deep spiritual significance. The cleaning gospel was entrusted in the hands of our lord. The cleaning process has to do with a full and accurate knowledge of the word. Not all hearers have the ability to be thus cleaned even after listening to the word. The heart must be fully attuned to revelation in the word. Only after being fully clean can we become cleaners.

John 15:3 Now ye are clean through the word which I have spoken unto you.

Matured fathers of the church are the pastors and teachers; having the same mind as Christ (1Cor 2:16); we are bearers of THE TIME and DIRECTION gospel which is in the horizontal gospel. Be mindful that Sons of God are not only inclined to walk in a perfection of works but also must be able to read the spiritual times, being set as watchers to the rest of the people in every age (Jer 4:16).

2.1.1 Specialization in the gospel

IN THE EARLY CHURCH, certain offices and positions were specially formulated with an organizational pattern suitable for the work of the gospel. This was a continuation of what the lord had put in place during his own ministry. For example Peter, James and John were always solicited for organizing his special outings and were always present with him during his special moments. Judas was the group treasurer and did help the ministry with reservation to compile their financial affairs. Peter was often assigned to special missions which were never handled by any other disciples. John was a close aid.

> *Luke 22:8-9 And he sent Peter and John, saying, Go and prepare us the passover, that we may eat. And they said unto him, Where wilt thou that we prepare?*

2.1.2 Talents within the gospel

The apostles were chosen from diverse socioeconomic backgrounds. Their ideas and contributions were put to proper use. Some were fishermen, tax collectors, and much later also doctor Luke etc. In our "modern day" we use the same principles and improve on them in order to have the best profiting for the church. A mixture of all into one family may pose questions in the flesh but such should not dissuade our focus on spiritual accomplishments.

2.1.3 Developing skills in the gospel

The ministry itself being a place where people get to be trained. Many people not only improve their spirituality but also their social, economic and academic potentials. They eventually fit in more beautifully into the society even if they started off as destitutes and or uneducated people. Involvement in Ministry is not about a person's education and social class but about the force and zeal to put the things of God at the first level of importance.

> *Acts 4:13 Now when they saw the boldness of Peter and John, and perceived that they were unlearned and ignorant men, they marveled; and they took knowledge of them, that they had been with Jesus.*

The end result of followership with the gospel of our lord 14 is that they end up improved, enabled strengthened, focused, revised and a lot better than they were in the past. The promise of God about our victory is in all things as long as we maintain his methods.

2.2 GOSPEL ENTITLEMENTS

> *John 15:15 Henceforth I call you not servants; for the servant knoweth not what his lord doeth: but I have called you friends; for all things that I have heard of my Father I have made known unto you.*

Talents are important but not indispensable in selecting actors of the different ministry entitlements. Therefore, our responsibility is to use all talents and blessings. We thank the lord for the activated gifts for specialization in ministry (Eph 4:11). The Holy Spirit actually participates in such work when all other apparent affiliations are not become an obstacle. Seeking and producing only results. We are friends with the lord because he assigned us to his own duties (John 15:15). Specialization helps us perform at our very best. There is no particular duty that is greater than the other in the house of God. Rather the quality of our work becomes the distinguishing factor.

The only reason God made hierarchy is because there is need for order. Someone is sent to give instructions in the name of the lord. Generally, people are given higher assignments when they prove their humility and meekness in spirit. The teacher therefore is the humblest.

> *John 13:13-14 Ye call me Master and Lord: and ye say well; for so I am. If I then, your Lord and Master, have washed your feet; ye also ought to wash one another's feet.*

By our sanctification, we are one with the lord **(Heb 2:11)**. In any household, there are variety of children. We are spiritual priests and kings **(Rev 1:6)**. We possess different ministry gifts in various proportions. Each one of us has a specialization. As we see here, Jesus had every ministry gift but was specialized as a teacher. He was best known by all as rabbi or raboni.

Entitled responsibility by the type of calling will have the teacher at the leading position assisted by pastors and the apostles, evangelists and prophets as collaborators. Although revelation is carried by the teacher, the pastoral ministry is the pivot of Christian ministry all over the world.

Gospel entitlements refer to the different specialised offices as designated by our lord in scripture to move his church towards a spiritual excellence and perfection. We distinguish these offices from those aimed at positioning men in places of honour with no relevance to seeking the face of God and pushing forth his kingdom. Jesus referred to us as disciples or apprentices. **Whatever Jesus did and represented in his ministry must be reproduced by us.**

2.2.1 JESUS IS AN APOSTLE (ADMINISTRATOR)

> *Heb 3:1 Wherefore, holy brethren, partakers of the heavenly calling, consider the Apostle and High Priest of our profession, Christ Jesus; 3:2 Who was faithful to him that appointed him, as also Moses was faithful in all his house. 3:3 For this man was counted worthy of more glory than Moses, inasmuch as he who hath builded the house hath more honour than the house.*

Jesus is an administrator inspires us to this calling. The overall apostle and strategist. Apostles are the church administrators and managers just as were Peter, James and John. Jesus was the chief administrator of all the church; he did this first through the disciples; teaching them this administration by example. Serving them. It is important to God that we lead others by example. Not making his word empty.

An apostle is one who maintains company with the lord. We see in scripture how the lord was glad that the apostles stayed with him through his trying moments. Staying together with other believers for as long as is necessary is an activity of the apostolic calling. This simple but persistent action is very important for the church. Jesus is the lead apostle being glued to the work at the front. Following the lord always was not easy in the days of our lord, neither is it easy today, there is reward for doing this (**Matt 19:28**).

Matt 19:28 And Jesus said unto them, Verily I say unto you, That YE WHICH HAVE FOLLOWED ME, in the regeneration when the Son of man shall sit in the throne of his glory, ye also shall sit upon twelve thrones, judging the twelve tribes of Israel.

2.2.2 JESUS A PROPHET (SPEAKER/PREACHER)

John 4:18 For thou hast had five husbands; and he whom thou now hast is not thy husband: in that saidst thou truly. 4:19 The woman saith unto him, Sir, I perceive that thou art a PROPHET. LET US AGREE ON THIS. Jesus our lord was undeniable the greatest of all prophets.

Jesus cautioned us to speak always words that will edify and transform for the better. This is because of the prophetic auction that is adorned to all believers. The new Testament believer is conceived towards a success and sanctification by uttered words. Speak always and say the right things. As Christians, we must speak blessings at every time even if we are not feeling like doing so. It is a calling of God after our lord Jesus Christ. In **Luke 9:54-56**, we see that Ministry can sometimes breed frustrations. The lord reminds us to remember to use our mouths correctly. There is something special about your words.

Luke 9:54 And when his disciples James and John saw this, they said, Lord, wilt thou that we command fire to come down from heaven, and consume them, even as Elias did? 9:55 But he turned, and rebuked them, and said, Ye know not what manner of spirit ye are of. 9:56 For the Son of man is not come to destroy men's lives, but to save them. And they went to another village.

2.2.3 JESUS AS AN EVANGELIST (EDUCATOR)

Matt 10:5 THESE TWELVE JESUS SENT FORTH, and commanded them, saying, Go not into the way of the Gentiles, and into any city of the Samaritans enter ye not: 10:6 But go rather to the lost sheep of the house of Israel. 10:7 And as ye go, preach, saying, The kingdom of heaven is at hand. 10:8 Heal the sick, cleanse the lepers, raise the dead, cast out devils: freely ye have received, freely give. 10:9 Provide neither gold, nor silver, nor brass in your purses, 10:10 Nor scrip for your journey, neither two coats, neither shoes, nor yet staves: for the workman is worthy of his meat. 10:11 And into whatsoever city or town ye shall enter, inquire who in it is worthy; and there abide till ye go thence. 10:12 And when ye come into an house, salute it. 10:13 And if the house be worthy, let your peace come upon it: but if it be not worthy, let your peace return to you. 10:14 And whosoever shall not receive you, nor hear your words, when ye depart out of that house or city, shake off the dust of your feet. 10:15 Verily I say unto you, It shall be more tolerable for the land of Sodom and Gomorrha in the day of judgment, than for that city. 10:16 Behold, I send you forth as sheep in the midst of wolves: be ye therefore wise as serpents, and harmless as doves.

TEN FEATURES OF EVANGELICAL PROCEDURE

i)   Jesus decides the exact number to go out; TWELVE

ii)   Jesus directs them targets where to go. ISRAEL 19

iii)   Jesus mentions where they should not go. GENTILES

iv)   Jesus identifies the kind of people they should talk to. LOST ISRAELITES

v)   Jesus gives content of their message. THE KINGDOM OF HEAVEN

vi)   Jesus gives an accompanying task HEAL SICK, RAISE DEAD, CLEANSE LEPERS, CAST DEMONS

vii)   Jesus gives instruction on modalities FREE OF CHARGE

viii)   Jesus tells them of their logistics. DIVINE PROVISION

ix)   Jesus gives the strategy. STAY WITH WORTHY ONES, SALUTE THEM, DEPART IF NOT RECEIVED

x)   Jesus talks about their attitude. WISE AND HARMLESS

The evangelist is not just someone who preaches the gospel to people. He is better described as the brain behind the success of all evangelical missions. Jesus is the wisest evangelist that ever lived. Reason why we are Christians today. Reason why the gospel cannot be stopped. However, today is another provision of the gospel and the Holy Spirit directs us with specific instructions for success.

2.2.4 JESUS IS A PASTOR (SHEPHERD)

Pastors are the ones that gather together the sheep. They identify the sheep by a character of similitude. These are they willing to execute the voice of the master. Such are always seasoned in the ways of the lord already. They protect the sheep from wolves.

> *Mark 14:27 And Jesus saith unto them, All ye shall be offended because of me this night: for it is written, I WILL SMITE THE SHEPHERD, AND THE SHEEP SHALL BE SCATTERED. 14:28 But after that I am risen, I will go before you into Galilee. 14:29 But Peter said unto him, Although all shall be offended, yet will not I.*

Shepherd care for the sheep. Sheep are the ones that hear the master's voice (shepherd). They are willing to do the same things that will fulfill the will of the lord. Many that walk in our mist as shepherds are wolves in sheep clothing.

2.2.5 JESUS IS A TEACHER

There is always one teacher at a time. The Holy Spirit has a special communication that he passes for a particular people and a particular time. The pastoral and teaching ministries are superior. Only people who are already seasoned with humility and meekness can occupy these functions. For the apostles, prophets and evangelists; these offices are committed to steadfastness and excellent discipleship.

> *John 3:1 There was a man of the Pharisees, named Nicodemus, a ruler of the Jews: 3:2 The same came to Jesus by night, and said unto him, Rabbi, we know that thou art a teacher come from God: .*

We have studied the five attributed and entitled ministry profiles of **Ephesians 4:11**. Find out in which of the five ministry entitlements you specialized in? Are you a visioneer? Then you should also position your followers to understand and walk with the best possible specialization that the lord has given them. Ministry gifts must all be used for services in the house of God.

2.3 ACT ON ENTITLEMENTS

The bible beckons on us in many scripture to HOLD FAST. This means there is a duty and responsibility that should be diligently put to task. These come from our ministry entitlements. Depending on how the lord has gifted the church, we have become either Apostles, prophets, evangelists, pastors or teachers **(Eph 4:11)**. These are the entitlements. Earthly titles are easy to see and to give. However, it is only after completing your responsibilities with the entitlements of the gospel that you receive a spiritual title. Do not start running after titles.

> *Eph 4:11-13 And he gave some, apostles; and some, prophets; and some, evangelists; and some, pastors and teachers; For the perfecting of the saints, for the work of the ministry, for the edifying of the body of Christ: Till we all come in the unity of the faith, and of the knowledge of the Son of God, unto a perfect man, unto the measure of the stature of the fulness of Christ:*

Women are not sanctified into the most Holy place **(Num 18:10)**. The teacher Paul reiterated this point that women must NOT teach in **1Cor14:34** (except under a teacher). In the new testament, the sanctuary is spiritual. The high priest is same as the teacher. I am a teacher and sanctified into the high priesthood. That is why I understand and should tell you all this without any doubting **Numb18:10** In the most holy place shalt thou eat it; every male shall eat it: it shall be holy unto thee.

Once you become a child of God, you receive the Godhead. Like Jesus, you become an apostle, prophet, and evangelist. No scripture segregates you from these offices. You are blessed with all spiritual blessings in heaven **(Eph 1:3)**. You do not need the word of another prophet to prosper in the earth; **2Chronicle 20:20** is not for you. You join also in the life of the prophetic. Beware of the false teachers ripping away your money saying they have anointing to prosper.

[[2Chron 20:20... Hear me, O Judah, and ye inhabitants of Jerusalem; Believe in the LORD your God, so shall ye be established; believe his prophets, so shall ye prosper]]. we see more in other books...

No ordinary man could say the things that Jesus said and did. Perfection ministry is a ministry of entitlements (see terms of references). We are here to do exactly what we are sent to do. Not to be polluted with titles. Far from that. 22 Jesus was never interested in earthly titles and honour. He was honoured at the end of his ministry with a BIG TITLE **(Eph 2:9-10)**.

Eph 2:9-10 Wherefore God also hath highly exalted him, and given him a name which is above every name: That at the name of Jesus every knee should bow, of things in heaven, and things in earth, and things under the earth;

Although a title confers respect from human institutions and seems relevant even in our Christian experience, entitlements give the owner a direction of command with spiritual importance. While it is not bad to honour elders in our society and people in their fields of natural work, this is not the place God has put them to minister spiritually. God positioned each believer to a duty for a later reward.

In other words, all that have titles also have entitlements and vice versa. However, like Jesus, we should honour others and let the lord honour us at the end. Titles confer honour to the holder but the first thing about the entitled is his/ her responsibility. There is something relevant that should be done only by you in this earth. Consider not failing to do it. While the title is relevant to the outside mind, the entitlement is about individuals.

After reading this book you must have a full account of your calling. Write it down and pull yourself to work. You are called by the lord to a ministry. That you must receive, understand and implement **(1Tim 1:12)**. Others can only train, monitor your growth and encourage you. Nobody can do this for you.

CHAPTER 3: Gospel titles

Christian Ministry Liabilities; what we don't need in ministry.

> *[[But it shall not be so among you: but whosoever will be great among you, let him be your minister; And whosoever will be chief among you, let him be your servant: Matt 20:25-]]*

3.1 GOSPEL TITLES

The term minister is not a title for earthly honour **(Matt 20:25)**. Gospel titles are liabilities of the lord's house and ministry. Titles prevail the most in an organizational set up that helps church leaders to bear fruit to themselves. These together agree not based on the spiritual results expected in the house of God but rather by a desire to acquire influence and affluence over other people. The bible asks us to flatter people with titles only when they are new converts. We start by studying the negative connotations of titles.

3.2 MISUSE OF GOSPEL ENTITLEMENTS

We just studied the five gospel entitlements **(Eph11:4)** which we also learnt in another series how they fall into the twofold ministry (vertical and horizontal). There are actually many people today named apostle, prophet, evangelist, pastor or teacher but who do not understand their terms of reference in the specialization they "boldly" have chosen to run.

Without the direction of the Holy Spirit, there is a high chance many have chosen these titles just to push forth their personal agendas. There are actually many "men of God" pretending to be something they are not called to be. Many of them are concerned to see that their titles give them honour before men and not the entitlement which describes their particular duties.

As such many of them scramble to be called apostle and prophet for example. They do not realize that the teacher has a higher calling in gospel specialization. This has nothing to do with miracles, signs and wonders as we recall in John the Baptist **(John10:41)** who was declared the greatest by our lord but performed no single miracle.

3.2.1 TITLED AS PRIESTS

When you study the bible and see the meaning of the word priest, there is every reason to pity anyone moving round with this title. The priest is a description of a type of person. Today, this title simply distinguishes them that fellowship with the father in praise or not.

Therefore, they that are born again exercise a spiritual priesthood. I have discussed elsewhere that the spiritual priesthood is actually a notion of sanctification (separation). Salvation is the first level of spiritual sanctification when a man becomes born again.

The second level of sanctification is gotten when such a person goes ahead to preach the gospel. This typical second level is what is referred to as priests in the Old Testament but it is a generic term in the new Testament given that we do not reside in a worldly sanctuary. The third and final sanctification is the teacher or high priest. This third sanctification is a calling of the lord and is tied to a special dispensation to receive truth and carry revelation.

Rather than call yourself priest to classify your duties in the house of the lord, study and adopt a biblical entitlement instead. In praise we have fellowship and dwelling with the lord. Everyone according to the sanctification or his level of initiation into the fellowship. It makes no sense actually to be called a priest in a Christian assembly just as it makes no sense to be called a "banana eater" amongst monkeys.

3.2.2 THE BISHOPS

In bible time, followers of Jesus waited some three years to become trained and acquainted with the ministry. This was a period of experience and learning particularly on the first three ministry entitlements. They learnt to be apostles, prophets and to become great evangelists. Each of these gifts were imparted into their separate ministries even if they were more effective only in some areas.

When you read the bible, you realize that the teacher Paul asked Timothy to ordain bishops at every stop point of ministration. This bishop was a focal person or what we call a "head boy" and not a leader as such. You cannot preach to someone in one instance and immediately produce a leader out of that person.

The office that many people occupy today as bishops is not a ministry entitlement but just a title to cause influence towards others. If you go to install a factory in a far-off country, you will take contacts of people on your first landing. It doesn't make such persons a full part of your team as of yet. This office biblically is ideally taken by people of lesser spiritual instruction.

3.2.3 THE ARCHBISHOPS

The archbishops denote the super titles and suppressed entitlements of the bishopric office. The bigger the title, the smaller the entitlements.

3.2.3 DEACONS

Like the bishops, deacons are provisional leaders for following up of new converts. It does not mean that they are ministry leaders. They are elders "in the flesh" who are yet to receive accurate spiritual direction.

3.2.4 ARCHDEACONS

The archdeacons denote the super titles and suppressed entitlements of the deaconate.

3.3 FALSE MINISTRY OFFICES

Before receiving or attributing titles, reflect on scripture. This is very important. All these offices and many others do not have a positive biblical inspiration and therefore are not a part of our Christian offices.

> *Matt 20:25-27 But Jesus called them unto him, and said, Ye know that the princes of the Gentiles exercise dominion over them, and they that are great exercise authority upon them. But it shall not be so among you: but whosoever will be great among you, let him be your minister; And whosoever will be chief among you, let him be your servant:*

The term arch was coined from the arch angels. This term which mainly has to do with authority flow is not in submission to the lord. In the earth, we do not need such fights and ramblings for bossing others. These instead put us down spiritually. *· ARCHBISHOP · YOUR LORDSHIP · ARCHDEACON · YOUR WORSHIP · PRIESTS · YOUR EMINENCE · ARCH DUKES · MOST VENERATED · NIGHTS etc · HIS HOLINESS/GRACE*

Such appellations must be discouraged. God's word is our guide and instructing instrument. Seek therefore ONLY to be entitled **(Eph 4:11)** in the ministry of our lord, do not go for the titles for to be honoured by men.

Do not shun from the entitlements namely; apostle, prophet and evangelist. You learnt what it takes to be one in the last chapter. When you receive any of these entitlements, the next thing is to be dedicated for service in that office. Do not choose any office to fain affection.

Finally, the term bishop should be retained mostly when describing both location of the one named and also the level of growth of a church in a location. We see this soon.

Acts14:23 And when they had ordained them elders in every church, and had prayed with fasting, they commended them to the Lord, on whom they believed.

Always fast and pray before giving titles, dedication of entitlements is a feasting because we are sure the lord is already at work when we see his gifts manifesting. You can ordain anybody anytime by laying on of hands. However, do not dedicate a vessel that is not sanctified by God. A sanctified vessel will manifest the gifts of the Holy Spirit.

False entitlements are not the same as bad followers or disciples. Bad disciples are those that after dedication to the lord's service, allow distractions to set in **(Luke 8:14)**. Instead of looking up to the lord Jesus as their standard, they instead start an unholy competition of prosperity. They take after Judas Iscariot. Their ministry too is annulled and given to another.

Ministers are a subset of the sanctified. A minister is a servant of the servants of God **(Matt 20:25)**. Not the many prosperity thieves amongst you. They steal from you and promise you earthly riches, being punished by God to believe in their own false teaching **(2Thes 2:11)**. Like the son of perdition (Judas Iscariot) who loved money more than his own brothers, they are revealed to you as it should be in this end time **(2Thes 2:3)**. I warn you again to beware of the wolves in sheep clothing.

CHAPTER 4: THE bishopric Office

headBoys?

> The future : Official colour sky blue

4.1 Bishops are geographical actors

A conventional bishop is never transferred; he/she can only be replaced. If his/her services are needed elsewhere as he grows in the word this must be as a result of a dedication. He/she may then become an apostle, a prophet or evangelist depending on how the lord wishes to use him or her. Eventually such (if male) can become a pastoral bishop and assigned as a shepherd to God's people.

Becoming a pastoral bishop means he goes back to his original pasture. The teacher Paul explained detailly the characteristics to be sought for when looking for a conventional bishop. Paradoxically many "bishops" of today are "high ranking spiritual men who are indeed dwelling in the flesh".

As God defines them from the bible, the conventional bishop is a provisional office aimed at laying the groundwork for evangelism. It should not be the typical high spiritual offices of our day. Dedicated bishops (apostolic and pastoral) on the other hand are spiritual leaders.

> *Titus 1:5 For this cause left I thee in Crete, that thou shouldest set in order the things that are wanting, and ordain elders in every city, as I had appointed thee: 1:6 If any be blameless, the husband of one wife, having faithful children not accused of riot or unruly. 1:7 For a bishop must be blameless, as the steward of God; not selfwilled, not soon angry, not given to wine, no striker, not given to filthy lucre;*

Don't hesitate therefore to appoint a conventional bishop. You have the opportunity to replace such as time goes on. There are actually many people that functioned at one time or other in the office of bishop but never earned an entitlement and eventually the pastoral bishop office.

Bishops are earmarked when the ministry spreads to other lands and territories **(Titus1:5-7)**. These are the potential pastors of the church in these places on reserve for any kind of misconduct on their part. Bishops are morally upright people; not necessarily skilled in the doctrine of righteousness **(Heb 5:13)** as are the ministry leaders (apostles, evangelists, prophets, teacher and pastor).

We have also the elders who are the bishop's associates. They make up the team that should uphold the word and testimony of Christianity in new fields.

> *1Timothy 3:1 This is a true saying, If a man desire the office of a bishop, he desireth a good work. 3:2 A bishop then must be blameless, the husband of one wife, vigilant, sober, of good behaviour, given to hospitality, apt to teach; 3:3 Not given to wine, no striker, not greedy of filthy lucre; but patient, not a brawler, not covetous; 3:4 One that ruleth well his own house, having his children in subjection with all gravity; 3:5 (For if a man know not how to rule his own house, how shall he take care*

of the church of God?) 3:6 Not a novice, lest being lifted up with pride he fall into the condemnation of the devil. 3:7 Moreover he must have a good report of them which are without; lest he fall into reproach and the snare of the devil. 3:8 Likewise must the deacons be grave, not doubletongued, not given to much wine, not greedy of filthy lucre; 3:9 Holding the mystery of the faith in a pure conscience. 3:10 And let these also first be proved; then let them use the office of a deacon, being found blameless. 3:11 Even so must their wives be grave, not slanderers, sober, faithful in all things. 3:12 Let the deacons be the husbands of one wife, ruling their children and their own houses well. 3:13 For they that have used the office of a deacon well purchase to themselves a good degree, and great boldness in the faith which is in Christ Jesus.

4.2 DEACONS

Deacons are better defined in most published books than are conventional bishops. However, in many churches, the deacons are placed high as assistants to preachers of the word. They are also appointed volunteers in a geographical area from our biblical records. Like the bishops, their ordination follows a strict morality enquiry.

From the biblical point of view, all Christians are disciples of Jesus. Once a person receives Christ and is born again, such a person should be ordained as a deacon alongside the bishops that is if he/she desires that office (**1Tim3:1**). They will then be assigned counselling duties in their respective domains while growing in the word. When a deacon proves him/herself competent, then they are qualified to carry out bigger functions (**1Tim 3:13**). Deacons should have different specializations. They can minister as counsellors in different aspects of church affairs. Some deacons should specialize also in Christian Ministry Organization (interpreting this book) so that they can counsel other deacons as they join into the church.

1Tim 3:13 says after a man performs well in the office of a deacon, such purchases a good degree. The deacon is not supposed to be someone necessarily learned in the things of God. Rather, a willing vessel in the hands of God (after receiving the first sanctification or salvation). Unfortunately, there are some that offer lip service to the lord declaring submission to him but their hearts are still lagging far behind. Like Judas Iscariot, such will eventually be put away (Acts 1:20). This should not be a problem to you.

> *Acts 1:20 For it is written in the book of Psalms, Let his habitation be desolate, and let no man dwell therein: and his bishopric let another take.*

It was in the effort to put moral and doctrinal order and decency to the different groups of believers that the teacher Paul kept sending letters. He had to select the best of them to put in positions of command although this in itself was not a sign that they were spiritually mature. Many of them were languishing in immorality (1Cor5:1-6). As concerns the teacher Paul, the best synonym for bishop will be a "headboy" of a learning school. Never forget they are still your pupils, though their heads should swell about their spiritual ability.

The teacher Paul however (having the mind of Christ) can judge these ones (1Cor 5:3). Note that his letter is addressed to Christians. These "Christians" are doing worse things than unbelievers do. They are champions at wrong doing. Christian ministry organization is important in all churches for the purpose of educating the ones that should grow to take leadership positions in the future.

> *1Cor 5:1 It is reported commonly that there is fornication among you, and such fornication as IS NOT SO MUCH AS NAMED AMONG THE GENTILES, that one should have his father's wife. 5:2 And ye are puffed up, and have not rather mourned, that he that hath done this deed might be taken away from among you. 5:3 For I verily, as absent in body, but present in spirit, have judged already, as though I were present, concerning him that hath so done this deed, 5:4 In the name of our Lord Jesus Christ, when ye are gathered together, and my spirit, with the power of our Lord Jesus Christ, 5:5 To deliver such an one unto Satan for the destruction of the flesh, that the spirit may be saved in the day of the*

Lord Jesus. 5:6 Your glorying is not good. Know ye not that a little leaven leaveneth the whole lump?

The Bishops that work normally have the soon-to-be position of an apostle in training (they need the practical word to complete this training) and their assistants are the deacons and they themselves (deacons) are also in training.

4.3 APOSTOLIC BISHOPS

As discussed, the apostolic bishops represent a growing conventional bishop. In a small church, the lead apostle may also function as the Pastoral Bishop while the assistants are the elders in their roles. The function of this bishop and elders IN BIG CHURCHES is mainly to;

1) Counsel and advice the believers. Converts are encouraged to stop by for their different issues to be addressed.

2) Coaching young people and training them to find their right calling in ministry.

3) As territorial leaders (no matter their growth) unless replaced, bishops administer the Benediction.

4) Together, they receive the evangelists during all outreaches in their catchment zones.

5) They are champions in right talking (they hail Christians, their lips never curse) Their reports are channelled to the permanent secretariat or branch pastor of the field. Their office is open to the public daily. The church should train such on different counselling technics.

- ❖ Marriage counselling
- ❖ Team counselling
- ❖ Vocational counselling
- ❖ Peace counselling
- ❖ Doctrinal counselling etc

The apostolic bishops generally should be able to handle other important church functions as in their terms of reference particularly in administration.

4.4 THE PASTORAL BISHOPS

These are the shepherds or branch pastors of their geographical zone. They are called by the lord after having proved themselves in season and through diverse tests. They are able to pursue important themes and coordinate church activities with a deserving spiritual touch. Their duties are as outlined in the terms of reference for pastors and branch pastors. Not all pastors are bishops because bishops and assistants are more about a location and longevity. Every pastor meditates the benediction. It is their duty to deliver this great service to the local churches **(Num 6:22- 27)**. See more details in book "Symbolic feasts of perfection".

CHAPTER 5: Gospel teacher

Christian Ministry Organizers

The teacher receives revelation;

What is God saying For

a PEOPLE

A PLACE and

a TIME

DISPENSE THE WORD OF THE SPIRIT.

Official colour white and black.

THIS IS **THE WATCHER (JER 4;16-17)**

[[For though ye have ten thousand instructors in Christ, yet have ye not many fathers: for in Christ Jesus I have begotten you through the gospel.1Cor 4:15]]

5.1 THE VISION BEARER OR TEACHER

We have studied on the teacher very detailly elsewhere in the parent book of this series. This entitled calling is the highest but humblest of all the ministry offices. The teacher is someone who is called by God and who carries a special message for a time, a people and for direction. In ministry setting, the teacher is also a pastor and central to ministry action. As such, Perfection ministry classifies this entitlement to the Permanent secretariat as with the Branch pastors.

Phil2:5 Let this mind be in you, which was also in Christ Jesus:

A vision bearer is someone who lives the word and has been trained by God to have the mind of Christ. He therefore is relaying the message of the Holy Spirit to the church because he listens and understands the Holy Spirit perfectly. When you have the mind of Christ, you can judge right because you judge yourself first with the word of God before you do others. This entitlement, I received from the lord and work hard everyday to help the church grow unto his perfection.

1Cor2:15 But he that is spiritual judgeth all things, yet he himself is judged of no man. 2:16 For who hath known the mind of the Lord, that he may instruct him? BUT WE HAVE THE MIND OF CHRIST.

Teachers are the church fathers not by age but by the mandate of God and should be listened to with all attention. The teacher Paul cautioned Christians not to follow just anyone. That they will have one father at a given time. There shall be many others preaching the gospel but only one person shall be raised as a father in the church.

1Cor 4:14 I write not these things to shame you, but as my beloved sons I warn you. 4:15 For though ye have ten thousand instructors in Christ, yet have ye not many fathers: for in Christ Jesus I have begotten you through the gospel. 4:16 Wherefore I beseech you, be ye followers of me.

5.2 TERMS OF REFERENCE/ TEACHER

VISION BEARER

- ❖ Is head of all ministry symbol and vision according to instruction of the Holy Spirit.
- ❖ Represents the effecting ministry in all matters concerning its life
- ❖ Proposes and implements themes and options that improve the life of the ministry.
- ❖ Has no running budget (runs via a PS)
- ❖ Concerned mainly with the horizontal gospel (meat Gospel)

Teachers are bound to exert authority in the fellowship in the name of the lord. All teachers are likened unto Christ Jesus who was not just a disciple (follower), rather he taught others to follow. Teachers are the trainers of trainers after Christ. The pastors are the trainers. Teachers actually don't exist on their own credit. The credit of all their work (message, timing, responsibility) goes to the Holy Spirit. God calls those who can handle this.

The vision bearer is also a pastor although he may double as a teacher by calling. The roles of this entitled calling will be disputed by spirits in opposing teachers. Terms of reference for this responsibility need not be over emphasized. The role of a teacher is essentially coordination. Believers need not think beyond helping this role to be smoothly run by the servant(s) of God to the office(s) entitled by God himself **(Eph 4:11)**.

In the New Testament, the Holy Spirit comes to each and every child of God separately. It is not like the OT where all the sanctified were supposed to stay together in a physical location or worldly sanctuary in order to be with and serve God **(Heb 9:1-18)**. As soon as you receive the gift of the Holy Spirit, you are assigned to your own mission, your own ministry.

There are some people who think serving God is about belonging in one "church organization" or the other. It is true that certain churches have structures that permit all their members to work in the ministration and expansion arms of ministry but this is not clearly understood.

Although you are a part of a ministry, you are expected to grow your own ministry by entitlement if you are listening to the Holy Spirit. There comes a time when He wants you to join a different chariot and move to another field (John 3:8). That is why this book comes to help you nurse and grow your own ministry from scratch.

This does not mean you must fall away with your parent assembly. No. You should start a fellowship in your house or neighbourhood. Your money cannot do your share of ministry. You have a mission to preach and teach the same gospel as Jesus Christ. You must do it by yourself in appreciation to God.

To earn greatness (**Matt 5:19**) and riches in heaven (**Mark 10:21**) you will do all these things by yourself. Men will testify about you being a follower of Jesus Christ. Do not be too busy with the things of this world. You are a spirit being after God. The kingdom we build is not flesh and blood. People need the message of Jesus everywhere to be trans formed. Endless celebrations as in some churches cannot help change lives.

> NB: Many people have been transplanted by their very hearts. Having problems with the heart, there was another healthy heart for them to use. After the operation, they did not stop loving their own wives and family because they received the hearts of other people. My friends the spirit of man has nothing to do with the flesh. Treat your heart to the discipline of God's kingdom. Two blood brothers may are complete strangers in the spirit as long as one of them refuses to allow influence from the word of God.

5.3 CHURCH GROWTH BY GENERATIONS

As soon as we start implementing this vision, we forget about who brought forth the vision (teacher). The teacher is like the one that planted (1Cor 3:6). He becomes the PS as soon as this planting is finished, to water alongside the others. He plays the same role as do all Branch Pastors. That is why this book helps the reader to discover and receive entitlements.

> *1Cor 3:3 For ye are yet carnal: for whereas there is among you envying, and strife, and divisions, are ye not carnal, and walk as men? 3:4 For while one saith, I am of Paul; and another, I am of Apollos; are ye not carnal? 3:5 Who then is Paul, and who is Apollos, but ministers by whom ye believed, even as the Lord gave to every man? 3:6 I have planted, Apollos watered; but God gave the increase. 3:7 So then neither is he that planteth any thing, neither he that watereth; but God that giveth the increase. 3:8 Now HE THAT PLANTETH AND HE THAT WATERETH ARE ONE: and every man shall receive his own reward according to his own labour. 3:9 For we are labourers together with God: ye are God's husbandry, ye are God's building. 3:10 According to the grace of God which is given unto me, as a wise masterbuilder, I have laid the foundation, and another buildeth thereon. But let every man take heed how he buildeth thereupon. 3:11 For other foundation can no man lay than that is laid, which is Jesus Christ.*

It does not matter whether you are in a Christian church or not. What matters is that you love the truth and want God glorified. We have received individual ministries (**1Tim1:12**) and should function in them by entitlements and not by titles (**1Cor3:5**). The objective is that we stay grounded in a truth that is received and that we can trace the fellowship of the believers by generations.

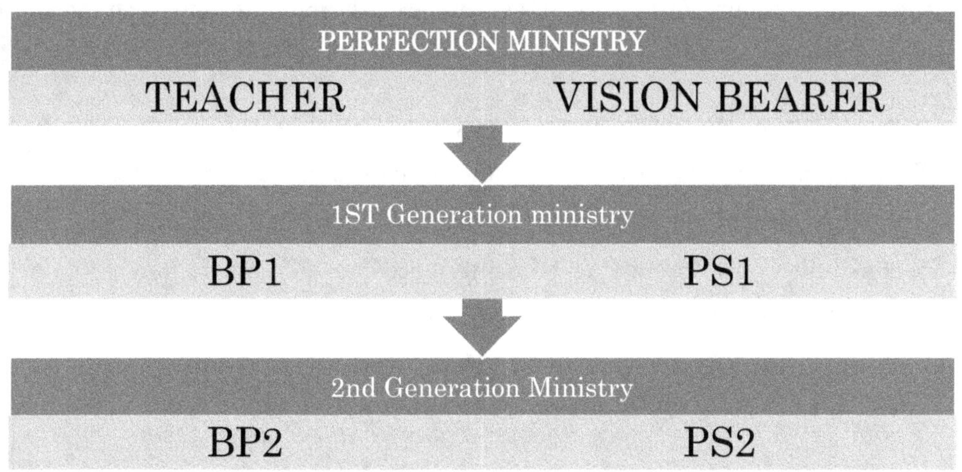

NB: I have met a lot of folks who try to explain that many MoG today have done one wrong thing or the other. As a result, they have stayed away from the churches. This is not funny. I tell you, when you do that, you are like the wicked servant that buried his talents in Matthew chapter 25:18.

God gave you knowledge about what the right thing to do should be. You decided to fold your hands, knowing that these MoG will go to hell. You did not show appreciation for your own salvation which the lord paid a high price for. That is a wicked thing to do with your gift. You must start doing something clear cut to improve the affairs of the kingdom of God from your church. This is not about joining any denomination. It is about learning about the love of God and spreading the message.

If you start sharing the love of God with others, the kingdom of God within you will multiply to the rest of the world. Otherwise, one day you will be sorry for doing nothing. Someone needs to hear what you heard from Jesus. He /she too can become as you are now.

This book propels you to the position of starting a Christian ministry even today. In this vision, you may one day play the role of branch pastors (BPs). If you are already a practicing Christian it is possible that you get dedicated in a short time. Otherwise you may enter into the titled ministry and be groomed unto spiritual life. You then proceed to reach out to the rest of the world with the saving message of our lord as well as the growth messages for the newly converted.

The churches from a point of influence spread in generations of BP/PSs. See the table. Read the message of **(1Cor 3:3-11)** and understand. The lord wants things to go in the direction of his influence. I do not hold credit for anything herein. I take responsibility only for letting Him influence me. For his influence, I am ready to spend all my life working for this lively hope that is in Christ Jesus, the lord.

> *Psalm 119:99 I have more understanding than all my teachers: for thy testimonies are my meditation. 119:100 I understand more than the ancients, because I keep thy precepts. 119:101 I have refrained my feet from every evil way, that I might keep thy word. 119:102 I have not departed from thy judgments: for thou hast taught me. 119:103 How sweet are thy words unto my taste! yea, sweeter than honey to my mouth! 119:104 Through thy precepts I get understanding: therefore I hate every false way. 119:105 NUN. Thy word is a lamp unto my feet, and a light unto my path.*

The mindset of all teachers is inundated by and with the word.

This same tradition I give to you by my ministry. That you also go ahead and influence others as the lord has done all of us. It is his will that we flourish in doing the right things **(Psalms 119:99-105)**.

We have underlined the Terms of reference of a teacher and vision bearer. Study the teacher more detailly in the book "Natural vertical and horizontal Gospels. The vision bearer (VB) who in branches is the Permanent secretary (PS) puts in place the expansion structures and the ministration structures; the branch pastor therefore plays the same role.

- ❖ EXPANSION STRUCTURES are the secretariats held by appointed pastors of the vision.
- ❖ MINISTRATION STRUCTURES (local) are the apostolic, prophetic and evangelistic functions.

Finally my role as a teacher (VB) is to let believers know the father's will. It is henceforth up to you to implement it and be rewarded. The ones that received many stripes are them that will read a book like this one and remain indifferent (Luke 12:47-48). Therefore, take heed to do all that is required of you. I am called to sow in the teaching ministry see that in the same revelation you toil for the lord. As the lord, I adopt the leadership principle of service **(1John4:36).**

"A leader is not a ladder climber but a ladder maker" John Maxwell.

> *1 John 4:36 And he that reapeth receiveth wages, and gathereth fruit unto life eternal: that both he that soweth and he that reapeth may rejoice together. 4:37 And herein is that saying true, One soweth, and another reapeth.*

See that you do not sow and reap corruption. Sowing and reaping is about addressing each line of the transforming power in the revealed word of God.

CHAPTER 6: THE PASTORAL ministry

Shepherds

The pastors see that everyone is safe and well taken care of.

REVELATION AND SPIRITUAL SACRIFICE. This is the **watchman (Ezek 3:17).**

[[...Simon, son of Jonas, lovest thou me more than these? He saith unto him, Yea, Lord; thou knowest that I love thee. He saith unto him, Feed my lambs. John 21:15]]

6.1 PASTORAL MINISTRY

A pastor or sherpherd takes care of the lord's sheep. The pastor is called by the lord or trained by the teacher. This can be directly as was the case with Peter who loved the lord so hard. He wanted to please Jesus in everything but could not know just yet how to do this. A pastor is a former Apostle, prophet or evangelist who loves the lord particularly as with teachers. Pastors develop the skills of the master, imparted by the Holy Spirit with fellowship. Can sense danger. In Perfection ministry, pastors are either productive apostles, prophets or evangelists who are appointed unto multiple spiritual functions.

The pastoral ministry is a shepherding ministry. It acts as such to protect children of God from external harm and jeopardy. It is a genuine concern of God that every child of God receives shelter and spiritual direction in righteousness. This is a place for spiritual rest in journeyings on earth.

Jer 3:14 Turn, O backsliding children, saith the LORD; for I am married unto you: and I will take you one of a city, and two of a family, and I will bring you to Zion: 3:15 And I WILL GIVE YOU PASTORS ACCORDING TO MINE HEART, which shall feed you with knowledge and understanding. 3:16 And it shall come to pass, when ye be multiplied and increased in the land, in those days, saith the LORD, they shall say no more, The ark of the covenant of the LORD: neither shall it come to mind: neither shall they remember it; neither shall they visit it; neither shall that be done any more. 33:15 In those days, and at that time, will I cause the Branch of righteousness to grow up unto David; and he shall execute judgment and righteousness in the land. 33:16 In those days shall Judah be saved, and Jerusalem shall dwell safely: and this is the name wherewith she shall be called, The LORD our righteousness.

Levi is a priest by selection or calling but the kings (Judah) is not part of God's resident family where the lord dwells with Levi. Until knowledge is received **(Jer 33:15)** from the pastors the kings cannot dwell with the lord. The ministry of pastors is a special one in the church making kings out of Levites **(Rev 1:6)**. God has made us great because we received his word. By this we have the Holy Spirit, and no need for the ark **(Jer 3:16)**.

We will proceed to study the missionary engagements of the pastoral. The first thing to note is that it is about care.

6.2 TERMS OF REFERENCE: PASTORAL MINISTRY

6.2.1 PERMANENT SECRETARY PS

- ❖ Has the rank of a PRIME MINISTER
- ❖ Is CALLED by the LORD **(Jer 3:15)** THROUGH the vision bearer or BPs.
- ❖ Is head of ministry organization and programs
- ❖ Receives and treats all petitions related with doctrine and orientations of the ministry for appreciation by the vision bearer.
- ❖ Receives and proposes actions necessary to be taken when faced with contrary spiritual aggressions.
- ❖ Prepares letters for appreciation, reproaches or stating the position of the ministry concerning specific issues.
- ❖ Receives and treats reports from all ministry directorates. • Has a running budget
- ❖ Coordinates all administrative, preaching and educational matters giving feedback reports to the church

As we saw earlier, the vision bearer for the purpose of implementing the lord's vision for the entire church through perfection ministry, references with the PS of all other Christian churches. This organization helps for collaboration. Collaboration follows in all other spheres of the ministry particularly the RTS or tithes fellowship.

THE ROLE OF PASTORS: All BPs are operationally represented in the ministry as PSs. They create and appoint leaders to ministry and the dedicated offices which run alongside with the pastoral. These are; the apostolic, the prophetic and the evangelists.

TERMS OF REFERENCE: PASTORAL MINISTRY

6.2.2 SECRETARY of COMMUNICATION

- ❖ Has the rank of Secretary General
- ❖ Assist the PS
- ❖ Is CALLED by the LORD via the vision bearer.
- ❖ Is head of communication affairs (may be assisted by sub departments such as radio, TV, social media, etc. as the vision grows)
- ❖ Displays activities of the ministry with the intention of growing it in all its dimensions
- ❖ Has a running budget but not a salary
- ❖ Produces records and implements the ministry vision to the world.

Secretary generals are expected to receive all correspondences from branch pastors and treat them accordingly. Communication is a vital tool for ministry success and increase. This office helps to give full information in an official manner to all the relevant sectors helping them to conform to various exigencies. Perfection ministry expects the churches to relay information pertaining to all church activities both present and future. Such information when properly handled will ensure that other partners act with understanding and confidence reigns within and without the ministry.

Unlike evangelists that focus on growing the local church, the role of the BPs is to expand the vision to foreign lands. This is the one on mission. This role means BPs are at the centre of missionary work as well as shepherding. Understanding this book is a key means of success of the pastoral.

TERMS OF REFERENCE: PASTORAL MINISTRY

6.2.3 SECRETARY OF RESOLUTIONS

- ❖ Has the rank of SECRETARY GENERAL
- ❖ Assist the Permanent Secretary (PS)
- ❖ Is CALLED by the LORD via the vision bearer
- ❖ Sits in permanently as presiding president during conflicts concerning parties that are members of the ministry or other such matters (assisted by all senior members of the church)
- ❖ Directs the physical policies of the ministry
- ❖ Coordinates uniforms and decorations
- ❖ Communicates the internal policies of the ministry during events.
- ❖ Has a running budget but not a salary
- ❖ Validates reports on projects related with the ministry vision

Resolution of different conflicts and presenting appropriate responses to questions will enable a smooth growth of the churches. We therefore put in place a platform for the amicable display of a love in fellowship. Through our works of continuous discipline in righteousness, the world is able to see that Christ is in our midst.

The BPs should select from the dedicated entitled workers brethren to help accomplish these functions. Pastoral dedications could be for both ministration and expansion purposes. All dedicated persons should remain in dedicated services from the day they receive their dedication.

TERMS OF REFERENCE: PASTORAL MINISTRY

6.2.4 SECRETARY OF PRAYER

- ❖ Has the rank of SECRETARY GENERAL
- ❖ Assist the PS
- ❖ Is CALLED by the LORD via the vision bearer
- ❖ Draws the SPIRITUAL projects of the church and writes out spiritual proposals for evangelical work.
- ❖ Draws and puts up agendas for meetings and prayer reunions.
- ❖ Ensures through correspondences that prayer is being prioritized according to ministry requirements.
- ❖ Directs the spiritual policies of the ministry
- ❖ Communicates the internal spiritual goals of the ministry on a daily basis.
- ❖ Has a running budget but not a salary
- ❖ Conducts regular findings on the spiritual evolution of the church

The secretariat of prayer is able to make the entire church see resolve in prayer as the ultimate problem-solving instrument during the end times. We expect to see more troubles coming into the world. All sequenced prayers and fasting including praying for special events are all displayed methodically for a sustainable following by the whole ministry.

The BP is responsible for and head of the pastoral office and ministry, making use of the 25% offering for running costs. His appointed LA, LE and PO in their respective ministries under shepherding of the BP will manage each the 25% allocations.

The BP must have in mind that financial stewardship is a delicate and important aspect of his shepherding ministry. The lord wants us first of all to give to the ones we minister to. Jesus did not just multiply bread to feed the five thousand, he first of all exploited the natural options by asking his disciples to contribute to feed the crowds (Matt14:16). As a pastor, you should not dwell on abstract but think about concrete workable ideas to help the needy.

*Matt14:16 But Jesus said unto them, They need not depart; **give ye them to eat.***

TERMS OF REFERENCE: PASTORAL MINISTRY

6.2.5 BRANCH PASTORS

- ❖ Have the rank of MINISTER(S)
- ❖ Is CALLED by the LORD via the vision bearer
- ❖ Directs the ministry vision and represents the vision bearer in his/her scope of influence
- ❖ Is linked to the ministry through all the recognized ministry figures.
- ❖ Delegated offices are appointed as the case may be.
- ❖ They are otherwise called territorial ministers OR simply the ministry PASTORAL bishops.
- ❖ Appreciates all ministry figures and gives responsibility to other ministry leaders.

The same functions attributed to the VB and the PS are decentralised to all geopolitical zones of the world. The branch pastors therefore fulfill all ministry obligations by doing the same things that are revealed.

TERMS OF REFERENCE: PASTORAL MINISTRY

6.2.6 SECRETARY OF YOUTH

- ❖ Have the rank of SECRETARY GENERAL
- ❖ Is CALLED by the LORD via the vision bearer
- ❖ Directs ministry vision on youths
- ❖ Schedules organizes youth events
- ❖ Has a running budget but not a salary
- ❖ Receives correspondences from all affiliated youth organizations.
- ❖ Develop and shares programs on the subject of gender.

Youth shall be considered as the group of people that are still dependent on others for any kind of tangible support that can be identified and addressed in a comprehensive way. Pastoral branch bishops have higher portfolio than are their centralised secretariats except for the PS who is ranked higher. Branch pastors are supposed to invite their following to the same faith as is in the pioneering body. As pastor, always ask yourself if your leadership is about honour from men or about helping the word of God reach the ends of the earth.

All branch pastors are responsible for upholding the ministry vision on all platforms. They are also in charge of putting up the dedicated offices which we will study presently. They are therefore required to take diligence with the Holy Spirit to dedicate any members of their team. Remember the dedicated unlike the ordained cannot be fired.

TERMS OF REFERENCE: PASTORAL MINISTRY

6.2.7 SECRETARY OF GENDER VALUE PROMOTION

- Have the rank of SECRETARY GENERAL
- Is CALLED by the LORD via the vision bearer
- Directs ministry vision on Gender inclined topics.
- Schedules organizes women events
- Has a running budget but not a salary.
- Develop and shares programs on the subject of gender.
- This secretariat will liaise with the resolution secretariat to resolve any issues generated as a result of gender differences.

6.3 GENERATIONS OF FOLLOWERS OF CHRIST

1Cor 11:1 Be ye followers of me, even as I also am of Christ.

We have seen that the BPs and VBs are both entitled offices for followership. If I follow the teacher Paul, I'm following Jesus. This is the true church tradition. This confidence we have in one another's ministry. Every branch pastor in his own field is considered a Permanent secretary (PS). As his/ her following grows, he will put in place the same set up as in the parenting church. There will be continuous mentoring with the same love and the same hope. The church setting where there is always one "superstar" man of God at the top does not allow this church tradition to flourish.

Every branch corresponds directly with its founding church and not necessarily with the VB. It will birth limitless generations of churches. Branches contribute 10% offerings to the parenting churches for expansion work. The church thus never becomes individual businesses. The bond of perfection is love **(Col 3:14)**. Is the church/person you now follow behaving as Paul? **Hints 2Thes 3:6-11, 1Cor 9:18, Phil 3:17-19.**

> Appointments to ministry offices depends on population of churches. The BP gives the directives to the four ministry branches (pastoral, apostolic, prophetic and evangelists). The appointments should not exceed 10%. From all the church, only 10% of its members can be appointed and thus share of the offering. After this quota is exceeded at any time, any dedicated ministers should seek to work in the expansion ministry in another field if they so want to. Appointed ministers can also go to different fields on transfer by the BPs. All Christians (not yet appointed) however that fulfill the tithes mandate, can redeem tithes.

All BPs must use this book to extract all Information required for effective financial stewardship of resources in the house of God. Such must also be adequately versed with the tithe fellowship. A pastor is a watchman. A watchman cares for those inside not outsiders. When you call yourself a pastor, you have to teach in rebukes. Also, since the lord does not commit women to teach, only men are eligible for the position of BPs.

CHAPTER 7: THE APOSTOLIC ministry

Administrators

The Apostle is always seeking new ways to make things work out.

7.1 PRESENTING THE APOSTOLIC MINISTRY

The Apostolic ministry represents a social bargaining structure. They supervise and bring about a cordial atmosphere to empower ministry groupings. Apostles are mainly involved in ministrations that bring about numerical growth.

> *[[And Jesus said unto them, Verily I say unto you, That ye which have followed me, in the regeneration when the Son of man shall sit in the throne of his glory, ye also shall sit upon twelve thrones, judging the twelve tribes of Israel. Matt 19:28]]*

7.2 THE APOSTLES

Apostles are the Administrators of the vision. They are responsible for putting in place the ground work for daily ministration of kingdom verities to the saints. As such they have the following important characteristics;

1) Stand with the lord

To minister persistently requires encouragement and peer comfort. The word of God asks us to be glued together. Disunity does a lot of harm to the progress of God's work. The apostles are the chief supporters of a vision just as the lord ministered in the company of the twelve. It should not become a business where people only try to get a footing to employ themselves gainfully as is the case today. By this definition, every Christian does some apostolic work.

2) Financial administration

Financial and other resources of the ministry are managed by the apostles. Finances play an important role and should be well managed following set norms. Apostles should be able to classify and use tithes, offerings, and other givings according to biblical norms. A perfection ministry write-up on this is available.

3) Discipleship

Discipleship is about getting people to identify with the lord and connect to his ideals. This too is done by the apostles. They put in place a set up for follow up and for spiritual counselling of new converts. Christian discipline is one of the most important practical lessons needed by all new converts. They will encourage others to be at the right places and at the right time. There are places and habits that Christians must avoid completely.

7.3 TERMS OF REFERENCE: APOSTOLIC MINISTRY

7.3.1 L E A D APOSTLE

- ❖ Is appointed by the Branch Pastor.
- ❖ Has the position of Director
- ❖ Is head of all local ministry administration
- ❖ Reports to the ministry vision producing reports to be consumed through the corresponding pastoral head (if he/she is not the one).
- ❖ Proposes themes and options that can improve all under his/her administration. • Has a running budget but no salary
- ❖ Teaches the horizontal gospel (meat Gospel) and vertical

TERMS OF REFERENCE: APOSTOLIC MINISTRY

7.3.2 GENERAL FIN. ADMINISTRATOR (GFA)

- ❖ Has the rank of sub-director

- ❖ Is appointed by the branch pastor on proposal from the lead apostle.
- ❖ Is head of financial affairs (may be assisted by financial secretaries, treasurer and auditors as the case may be appointed by the lead apostle)
- ❖ Has a running budget
- ❖ Coordinates all financial matters and gives weekly reports to the hierarchy

The lead apostle is head of all apostolic work and carries out intense activities with all believers who are dedicated as apostles in the local church, holding regular meetings with them. He decides which of them is appointed to apparent apostolic offices according to 10% norms. He manages 25% running funds.

TERMS OF REFERENCE: APOSTOLIC MINISTRY

7.3.4 H U M A N RELA TIONS OFFICER (HRO)

- ❖ Has the rank of sub-director
- ❖ Is appointed by the branch pastor on proposal from the lead apostle.
- ❖ Is head of human affairs (may be assisted by some moral elders and advisers as the case may be; all appointed by the lead apostle)
- ❖ Has a running budget
- ❖ Produces reports on issues that concern all ministry personnel and things that animate the life of the ministry

TERMS OF REFERENCE: APOSTOLIC MINISTRY

7.3.5 PROJECTS AND BUDGET SUB DIRECTOR (PBD)

- ❖ Has the rank of sub-director
- ❖ Is appointed by the vision bearer on proposal from the lead apostle.
- ❖ Is head of local projects and budgeting (may be assisted by experts and key partners as the case may be appointed by the lead apostle)
- ❖ Has a running budget
- ❖ Produces reports on projects related with the ministry vision

Ministry apostles are grown by an adaptive mechanism such that newly dedicated apostles are attached to the fold by those already exercising in these duties. Their leaders must then make recommendations to the branch pastors concerning the growth of brethren in this ministry calling. They are eventually used to expand ministry through other internal or external networks.

The LA in the same manner as from his budget should allocate amounts to be managed in offices in his/her ministry area. Such allocations should not be subject to debate or lobbying

.

TERMS OF REFERENCE: APOSTOLIC MINISTRY

7.3.6 T I T H E S AND DISTRIBUTION OFFICER (TDO)

- ❖ These are the RTS ministry staff
- ❖ They collect all tithes and bank according to normal banking procedures
- ❖ They run the tithes and distribution
- ❖ They keep all records of the tithe
- ❖ They give reports to hierarchy as required
- ❖ They advise tithers and provide information about the RTS

NB Study the RTS Manual.

The tithes and distribution of resources according to stipulated guidelines;

- ❖ 90% of all tithes are shared equally to all tithers in perfection CMO adapted platforms,
- ❖ all the rest (9%)is shared equally to all church executives.
- ❖ After paying the tithe of the tithe (1%) to the RTS **(Neh 10 :38)**

This function is an auxiliary function adapted to the RTS project which is as written in the book titled "RTS Manual" and run throughout the earth. All churches are encouraged to register their Christians into the tithe distribution scheme as revealed. Perfection ministry partnerships will foster understanding of the tithe fellowship.

Summarized and key information on this is available online on the website perfectionministry.org. Reading the book "The Holy Spirit's Money" will also be of help to inform you of the impending importance of the tithe fellowship. Ensure that you get this information and share with all members of your church or group.

The question on how best to manage church finances is irrelevant to God as long as we do it in righteous judgement. God justifies a man the same way s/he justifies others. Let the churches use the money for all the most relevant needs and help their peers in meeting all goals of the church.

TERMS OF REFERENCE: APOSTOLIC MINISTRY

7.3.7 MINISTRY FINANCES Officer (MFO)

- ❖ These are motivated ministry staff
- ❖ They collect all offerings, seeds and partnerships to bank according to normal banking procedures
- ❖ They run the distribution of offering, and any other givings. All specific partnerships are deposited in the accounts for projects
- ❖ They keep all records of the finances in these domains.
- ❖ They give reports to hierarchy as required

TERMS OF REFERENCE: APOSTOLIC MINISTRY

7.3.8 INTERNAL/EXTERNAL H u m a n Relations Officers (HRO)

- ❖ These are motivated ministry staff
- ❖ They organize the protocol and other such tasks in the church
- ❖ They generate reports to be sent to the permanent secretariat through the lead apostle
- ❖ They keep all records of the finances in these domains.
- ❖ They link up with all other departments and insert resource needs into the general budget

TERMS OF REFERENCE: APOSTOLIC MINISTRY

7.3.9 COMMUNITY ASSISTANT (CA)

- ❖ They are motivated ministry staff
- ❖ They collect information that will help develop an equitable relationship with the community
- ❖ They arrange the external distribution activities and any other giving
- ❖ They keep all records of the external activities
- ❖ They give reports to hierarchy as required.

Running costs from offerings are run by the heads of each dedicated calling. They are attributed quarterly or by semesters and shared approximately as follows;

- ❖ 25% for the pastors, (BP or PS)
- ❖ 25% for the apostles, (LA)
- ❖ 25% for prophets (PO)
- ❖ 25% evangelists. (LE)

Such money is not paid out as salary but used to motivate staff, run activities or buy utilities. Costs for running the churches (rents and equipment) are borne from seeds and partnerships. This should be forwarded to the church through the projects office. Special donations will be solicited to perform particular tasks.

The lead apostle has the responsibility to coordinate and delegate functions to supplement the demands of the different arms of ministry while reporting to the PS. The financial policy of the CMO based on sound biblical behaviour should not in any case overide righteous judgement. Priority must be given to what is right rather than justice.

CHAPTER 8: THE prophetic ministry

Preachers/speakers

The prophet is champion of the vertical gospel.

DISPENSE THE SPIRIT OF THE WORD

> Official colour multiple colours; pink, purple, green, [illegible], grey, violet, brown for multiple gifts of prophecy

8.1 PRESENTING THE PROPHETIC MINISTRY

Prophets are involved in preaching ministrations that bring transformations. This ministry is key to all activities helping sinners to the house of God. It is headed by the prophetic overseer. Someone with great zeal for the house of God. 1Cor14:29 says there should be special people called to this office during our daily ministrations. This is the vertical ministration.

> *[[Let the prophets speak two or three, and let the other judge. If any thing be revealed to another that sitteth by, let the first hold his peace. 1Cor 14:29-30]]*

8.2 PROPHETS

The ministry entitlement of prophets is described by the teacher Paul in 1Cor14:29-30. These are the ones the lord uses to minister to the people. Prophets are sent to preach the vertical gospel and to make prophetic utterances for spiritual edification. This gospel brings new members into the family of God.

They generally carry the anointing to cause miracles, healings and other such graces so that people can believe and receive from God. The vertical grace of salvation supersedes all shadow graces.

The horizontal gospel is more important to God our father. Just like all parents towards their prime age (end time), God is more interested in growing his kids to maturity than making new ones. Many Christians are not unaware that without this spiritual growth, children don't have effective fellowship with the father.

No matter how anointed a prophet may be, they are still subject to the teacher. This is an unusual teaching in our day where a lot of people are travelling thousands of miles to have a prophecy. Every prophet is sent by God but unfortunately, many of them have not assimilated the word like the teachers. For this reason, they take in to carnal actions and many lose their way in the shadow prosperity gospel. Read the lead text on vertical and horizontal gospel to understand.

A child of God is one that judges himself daily and plans improving his life as a matter of strict urgency. God (father) is interested in Children who are like Jesus in all things. Who 67 value the gift of righteousness and put themselves constantly under checks and balances. Not ones that are complacent and keep compromising spiritual verities and overstretching the free gift of grace. Such grace is unable to conceal sin.

Matt 7:20 Wherefore by their fruits ye shall know them. 7:21 Not every one that saith unto me, Lord, Lord, shall enter into the kingdom of heaven; but he that doeth the will of my Father which is in heaven. 7:22 Many will say to me in that day, Lord, Lord, have we not prophesied in thy name? and in thy name have cast out devils? and in thy name done many wonderful works? 7:23 And then will I profess unto them, I never knew you: depart from me, ye that work iniquity. 7:24 Therefore whosoever heareth these sayings of mine, and doeth them, I will liken him unto a wise man, which built his house upon a rock:

Beware of falsifying your prophetic calling as many have done already. Those who will be addressing the lord as in **Matt 7:22** are seasoned prophets. They think they are serving the lord simply because they were anointed for works. The anointing is for service and not for self gain. Be not deceived, that the shadow gospel (prosperity) rewards all it's actors only in the earth.

NB: The spirit of "all prophecy" must have root in the word of God. It does not suffice to give prophecy. More important is that the word of God with full revelation carries the central theme of every prophecy. In the book "Textbook of the Christian prayer" we studied that all believers should prophesy. If we pray while prophesying as much as we should, there will be no need to do supplications for needs to the lord. We will meet our them at the appointed time and place. Let us see the terms of reference of prophets in the church.

8.3 TERMS OF REFERENCE: PROPHETIC MINISTRY

8.3.1 PROPHETIC OVERSEER

- ❖ Is appointed by the BP
- ❖ Has the RANK of Director
- ❖ Is head of preaching ministry •• Prepares messages and facilitates roles with other ministers
- ❖ Preaches mainly the milk/salvation gospel or vertical gospel
- ❖ Reports to the ministry vision producing reports to be consumed through the corresponding pastoral head (if he/she is not the one).
- ❖ Proposes PREACHING themes that are validated in the permanent secretariat for serial programmings.
- ❖ Has a running budget

TERMS OF REFERENCE: PROPHETIC MINISTRY

8.3.2 PROPHETIC COUNCIL (7 members)

- ❖ Are assistant or deputy POs.

- ❖ Appointed by the PS/BP on proposal from the PROPHETIC OVERSEER.
- ❖ Headed by the PO, they sequentially prophesy during church meetings and according to their manifested gifts.
- ❖ Is head of different divisions of the prophetic (may be assisted as the case may be, appointed by the prophetic overseer)
- ❖ Coordinates search for new messages with spiritual changes and events of the hour

The Prophetic Overseer in the same manner as from his budget should allocate amounts to be managed in offices in his/ her ministry area. Such allocations should not be subject to debate or lobbying.

TERMS OF REFERENCE: PROPHETIC MINISTRY

8.3.3 GENERAL S E C U R I T Y Officer (GSO)

- ❖ Has the rank of Sub director
- ❖ Is appointed by the PS/BP on proposal from the PO
- ❖ Is head of human security affairs
- ❖ Has a running budget
- ❖ Produces reports on issues that concern all ministry personnel and things that animate the security life of the ministry.

TERMS OF REFERENCE: PROPHETIC MINISTRY

8.3.4 D I R E C T O R OF TECHNICAL SERVICES (DTS)

- ❖ Has the rank of Sub director
- ❖ Is appointed by the PS/BP on proposal from the PO
- ❖ Is head of TECHNICAL services at all levels
- ❖ Has a running budget
- ❖ Produces reports on issues that concern equipment and resources for services such as sound, lighting, network etc

TERMS OF REFERENCE: PROPHETIC MINISTRY

8.3.5 PREACHING ADVISER (PA)

- ❖ Has the rank of CHIEF OF SERVICE
- ❖ Is appointed by the PO
- ❖ Is head of preaching material preparation for ministration
- ❖ Produces reports on projects related with the ministry vision

The prophetic overseer is head of all prophetic work and carries out intense activities with all believers who are dedicated as prophets in the local church, holding regular meetings with them. He decides which of them is appointed to apparent prophetic offices according to 10% norms. He manages 25% running funds.

TERMS OF REFERENCE: PROPHETIC MINISTRY

8.3.6 DELIVERANCE ADVISER (DA)

- ❖ Has the rank of CHIEF OF SERVICE
- ❖ Is appointed by the PO
- ❖ Is head of deliverance material preparation for ministration
- ❖ Produces reports on projects related with the ministry vision

TERMS OF REFERENCE: PROPHETIC MINISTRY

8.3.7 HEALING ADVISER (HA)

- ❖ Has the rank of CHIEF OF SERVICE
- ❖ Is appointed by the PO
- ❖ Is head of preaching material preparation for ministration
- ❖ Produces reports on projects related with the ministry vision

TERMS OF REFERENCE: PROPHETIC MINISTRY

8.3.8 CHURCH SECURITY DELEGATE (CSD)

- ❖ Has the rank of CHIEF OF SERVICE
- ❖ Is appointed by the PO
- ❖ Is head of church security and ushering preparation for ministration
- ❖ Produces reports on projects related with the ministry vision

Taking care of security requires close association with the apostolic ministry; with budgeting into the prophetic. The BP/PS should work out for this collaboration to be effective.

CHAPTER 9 : Calling of THE evangelists

Educators

The Evangelist as coaches and as mentors.

> *[[THESE TWELVE JESUS SENT FORTH, and commanded them, saying, Go not into the way of the Gentiles, and into any city of the Samaritans enter ye not: Matt10:5]]*

9.1 E FOR EDUCATORS

The believer should not be moved even by frequent church goers, true Christianity operates from a hidden position. Follow the prophecy of Rev 12. Spiritual children of God are not about church buildings and visible things.

> *Rev 12:17 And the dragon was wroth with the woman, and went to make war with the remnant of her seed, which keep the commandments of God, and HAVE THE TESTIMONY OF JESUS CHRIST.*

The true church of our God is a remnant of what you see flooding stadiums and auditoriums of men. Majority of them offer lip service to God. their hearts are busy planning to spend the blessings they can receive. They are not interested in the kingdom of God. The will of the father is the paramount thing to be on the safe side (Matt 7:21).

To fully exhibit the testimony of Jesus Christ, the teaching ministry is expanded and grounded by the ministration of evangelists. Nothing is taken for granted. The devil is the architect of the rampant false doctrines of our day. The evangelist therefore is that person who is searching scripture on a daily basis in order to understand revelation.

They then transmit such in the church as required under supervision of the teacher. It is a difficult spiritual thing to transfer and relate truth. With this difficulty, many assigned MoG have resigned to their own false version of truth (2Thes 2:11). The evangelistic followership is important for packaged truths to be transported. Someone has to learn in order to teach.

9.2 PRESENTING THE EVANGELISTIC MINISTRY

Evangelists are primarily involved in field work. Field work can be within other Christian ministries (teaching) or to unbelievers (preaching). They ensure that what is done by preaching and teaching yields lasting results. Though important for local ministration, particularly through music, this ministry is key to all expansion works. Just like the pastoral service, music is a pivoting role extending to all the others.

Every truth that comes to you becomes your responsibility. You have to stand by it and transmit it to the next believer. I see some foolish Christians sticking only with ideas of their special "man of God". Ignoring others as a code of conduct. It is therefore appropriate for believers to be educated in order to fit into this ministry office. Younger people are more generally better evangelical actors who then inspire others as they also participate in diverse activities. Evangelists are actors primarily of the outreach ministrations (1Cor3 :6).

> *1Cor3 :6-11* **I have planted, Apollos watered;** *but God gave the increase. So then neither is he that planteth any thing, neither he that watereth; but God that giveth the increase. Now he that planteth and he that watereth are one: and every man shall receive his own reward according to his own labour.*

For we are labourers together with God: ye are God's husbandry, ye are God's building. According to the grace of God which is given unto me, as a wise masterbuilder, I have laid the foundation, and another buildeth thereon. But let every man take heed how he buildeth thereupon. For other foundation can no man lay than that is laid, which is Jesus Christ.

9.3 TERMS OF REFERENCE: EVANGELISTS MINISTRY

9.3.1 LEAD EVANGELIST (LE)

- Is appointed by the BP/PS
- Has the RANK of Director
- Is head of EDUCATING ministry during church meetings
- Prepares messages from the vision archives and books (from teachers)
- Leading roles in external or outdoor events
- Preaches mainly vertical gospel but not limited
- Teach and train members
- Reports to the ministry vision producing reports to be consumed through the corresponding pastoral head (if he/she is not the one).
- Proposes TEACHING themes that are validated in the permanent secretariat for serial programming.
- Organize and run the cell system of the church
- Has a running budget but no salaries

Teachers are involved with the horizontal gospel which the evangelists relay to the church. They principally working in the part by nursing believers. Go out for local soul winning in different catchments. Like the lord, they mold others to go out and win sinners home. This ministry objectively covers the vertical dimension of ministry.

The evangelists have a holistic view to ministry as concerns expansion work being specialized in specific field aspects in that they mostly water what is planted by the teacher.

1Cor 3:6 I have planted, Apollos watered; but God gave the increase.3:8 Now he that planteth and he that watereth are one: and every man shall receive his own reward according to his own labour.

TERMS OF REFERENCE: EVANGELISTS MINISTRY

9.3.2 MUSIC DIRECTORS (3) (MD)

- ❖ Has the rank of SUB-DIRECTORS
- ❖ Is appointed by the PS on proposal from the LE.
- ❖ Coordinate and motivate choir activities
- ❖ Runs the "Perfection Music and Dance Centre" PMDC.
- ❖ Is head of different divisions of music (may be assisted as the case may be).
- ❖ Coordinates search for music inspiration and creation of talents in music, monitoring growth of such with changes in activities and events of the hour
- ❖ Copy reports to the secretary of prayer
- ❖ Has a running budget

Music is a very important accomplice of Christian ministration. This should be considered priority during spiritual engagements. Encouraging one another to become thankful to the lord at all times in singing and melody. It should be a way of life that believers continue instructing Christians to sing praises at all times. This area is led by the evangelists

Opportunities to scale up musical activities therefore should receive as much support as be. This ministry produces songs needed to minister to the people of God and to help them open their hearts to the word of God. Singing is praying in a special way. Perfection ministry encourages investments to improve the musical ministrations at all levels.

TERMS OF REFERENCE: EVANGELISTS MINISTRY

8.3.3 MISSIONS COORDINATOR (MC)

* ❖ Has the rank of CHIEF OF SERVICE
* ❖ Is appointed by the PS on proposal from LE
* ❖ Is head of EVANGELISTIC MISSIONS affairs
* ❖ Takes care of the youth and children ministry in field meetings
* ❖ Displays and distributes approved ministry tools
* ❖ PREPARES and budgets for missions after consultations
* ❖ Produces reports on issues that concern all ministry missions and things that animate the social life of the ministry

TERMS OF REFERENCE: EVANGELISTS MINISTRY

9.3.4 CRUSADES COORDINATOR (CC)

* ❖ Has the rank of Chief of SERVICE
* ❖ Is appointed by the PS on proposal of the LE.
* ❖ Is head of crusade technical preparation for ministration
* ❖ Provides all technical and administrative details ensuring that internal and external preparations are met.
* ❖ Produces reports on projects related with the ministry evangelisation vision

The LE in the same manner as from his budget should allocate amounts to be managed in offices in his/her ministry domain. Such allocations should not be subject to debate or lobbying.

TERMS OF REFERENCE: EVANGELISTS MINISTRY

9.3.5 TRANSLATIONS COORDINATOR (TC)

* ❖ Has the rank of Chief of SERVICE
* ❖ Is appointed by the PS on proposal from LE.
* ❖ Is head of translating Christian material preparation for ministration
* ❖ Organizes a translators forum and network

❖ Produces reports on projects related with the ministry vision

TERMS OF REFERENCE: EVANGELISTS MINISTRY

9.3.6 CHURCH RELATIONS COORDINATOR (CRC)
- ❖ Has the rank of Chief of SERVICE
- ❖ Is appointed by the PS on proposal from LE.
- ❖ Is head of preparation for linkage to other local Christian churches
- ❖ Keeps records of such relations and correspondences for references and improvement
- ❖ Produces reports on projects related with the ministry vision

The LE is head of all evangelical work and carries out intense activities with all believers who are dedicated as evangelists in the local church, holding regular meetings with them. He/she decides which of them is appointed to apparent evangelical offices according to 10% norms. He/she manages 25% running funds.

CHAPTER 10: RUNNING the MINISTRY

The muzzled OX

The muzzled ox

(taught from the Old to the New testament)

is the PILLAR TEACHING and guide

on Godly financial stewardship by ministers of the gospel.

The Levite that were sanctified, did not own property.

This is the sign of « our muzzling by sanctification ».

We too have been muzzled.

Any man that serves the lord in this capacity

(just as the ox),

should receive daily living benefits.

This is not the same as a salary;

living off the proceeds of the lords' church

when indeed we expect to be rewarded in heaven.

10.1 MORAL FINANCIAL CONDUCT

[[For yourselves know how ye ought to follow us: for we behaved not ourselves disorderly among you; 2Thes 3:7]]

There is both appropriate and bad conduct in finances. Running ministry budgets are derived primarily from offerings. This money is set forth for ministry expenses as a result of the "muzzled worker" phenomenon. Church leaders are not working for a salary. Our reward comes from God who will one day beckon on us to enter into his joy.

Let us not forget that so many that were called into ministry have passed on into eternal damnation. Often, this was as a result of seeking earthly reward (salary) for their services in the house of God. We cannot afford to do the same things they did (either in error and/or greed). The bad organizational and aggravating conduct or attitude started 2000 years ago.

Phil 3:17-19 Brethren, be followers together of me, and mark them which walk so as ye have us for an ensample. (For many walk, of whom I have told you often, and now tell you even weeping, that they are the enemies of the cross of Christ: Whose end is destruction, whose God is their belly, and whose glory is in their shame, who mind earthly things.)

Do not think that greedy workers in God's house are hiding in some distant forest. They are the same people you talk with and interact with on a daily basis but who for money reason(s) refuse to do the word of God. The bible tells us that God is not a respecter of persons. Do not go to hell because you choose to be deceived by others. Follow me well.

When I talk with many "pastors" for example about how tithes should be used by Christians, they reply that tithes are used for salaries to pastors and other such things. That is not biblical. You can read about tithes in my book "The Holy Spirit's Money" which many wicked and sneaky church leaders are avoiding even now. I warn you again "stay away from God's money".

10.2 HOW YE SHOULD BEHAVE

After reading the whole bible, I have not seen any passage saying that "people work on earth for God to be paid here". The nonsense of paying "pastors" salaries is what has grounded the Holy Spirit and turned many Christian churches into religions. Read **2Thes 3:6-12** and make your own notes. If you like, continue serving yourself; the reward you receive from this world is all you will get. Withdraw from them if you want to serve God. God said WITHDRAW (**2Thes 3:6**).

> *2Thes 3:6 Now we command you, brethren, in the name of our Lord Jesus Christ, that ye withdraw yourselves from every brother that walketh disorderly, and not after the tradition which he received of us. 3:7 For yourselves know how ye ought to follow us: for we behaved not ourselves disorderly among you; 3:8 Neither did we eat any man's bread for nought; but wrought with labour and travail night and day, that we might not be chargeable to any of you: 3:9 Not because we have not power, but to make ourselves an ensample unto you to follow us. 3:10 For even when we were with you, this we commanded you, that if any would not work, neither should he eat. 3:11 For we hear that there are some which walk among you disorderly, working not at all, but are busybodies. 3:12 Now them that*

are such... exhort by our Lord Jesus Christ, that with quietness they work, and eat their own bread. 3:13 But ye, brethren, be not weary in well doing

The tradition of our brother Paul was to work for his own expenses.

One thing that is never discussed but which is at the heart of the perversion of ministry is called salary. Salary is a full reward for the work you do. Paying a salary for the work of a spiritual God is wrong. God has always promised a reward for us. Where? In heaven.

Do not force the reward now. God did not employ anybody for "full time pastoring" job as far as the bible is concerned. Period. Go work your own private money elsewhere. Stop confusing children of God with your endless quests for money. Many organised religions are into this misleading unbiblical practice. For this reason, I have seen many lazy people moving up and down with bibles in ampits. A lot of them are worse than scammers. **Withdraw from salary churches.** Ministry is free of charge.

> *1Cor 9:18 What is my reward then? Verily that, when I preach the gospel, I may make the gospel of Christ without charge, that I abuse not my power in the gospel.*

10.3 THE RUNNING BUDGET

> *1Cor 9:7 Who goeth a warfare any time at his own charges? who planteth a vineyard, and eateth not of the fruit thereof? or who feedeth a flock, and eateth not of the milk of the flock? 9:8 Say I these things as a man? or saith not the law the same also? 9:9 For it is written in the law of Moses, Thou shalt not muzzle the mouth of the ox that treadeth out the corn. Doth God take care for oxen? 9:10 Or saith he it altogether for our sakes? For our sakes, no doubt, this is written: that he that ploweth should plow in hope; and that he that thresheth in hope should be partaker of his hope.*

You have just seen that every child of God should labour elsewhere for private money (enrichment). We must allow money collected in the churches to serve the purposes of God's dedicated workers **(1Cor 9:7)**. That is the running cost.

Churches are the spending ground for all offerings. Whatever budget is available should be utilized by the particular church to meet all daily expenses. We should not give responsibilities to our fellow brethren without providing them with means to accomplish their specific and diverse roles. This opinion is captured by the word of God.

> *1Cor 9:9 Thou shalt not muzzle the mouth of the ox that treadeth out the corn.*

Notice that the ox in this scripture is at work. This is not the same as a salary. A running cost is so that all the work done goes smoothly. A salary on the other hand decides whether the person earning it is satisfied. This is not the case with the running cost which is for the enduring group.

All appointed church leaders should never be subjected to any form of humiliation concerning their decisions to spend allocated budgets by group. Distributions by group should follow the 25% allocation plan. The BP, LA, LE and PO are responsible for management of allocated running funds and distributions to their peers. Each of these ministry branches should be created by the BP as the church increases in numerically.

Unlike money from tithes shared to all the sanctified, motivation money shared to dedicated ministry BP, LA, LE and PO and peers should be used for anything they want. They are as the ox that threadeth the field. Only money from offerings are used for this purpose. This money will also help them run group meetings and buy various utilities by group.

As much as possible, offerings should not be used for general costs. Partnerships can be mobilised to cover the this while offerings are used for the purpose of running the dedicated services. This may take the form of direct motivation to the ones having the entitlements. The lord does not want anyone struggling to do the labour alone. This does not mean that people should fight over these funds. There must be excellent order. Help is solicited if general funds do not meet needs.

10.3 TYPES OF COLLECTION:

No matter your financial status as a minister, do all the giving (entry points) so there will be enough to officially spend in the house of God.

i) Offering Thanksgiving (collection during regular meetings)

God has demonstrated the principle of the tithe in all collective activities. In Perfection ministry, tithe all your offerings from all branches. Send 10% to the parent church to run its expansion services. The rest of the money (90%) should be distributed following the 25% guidelines from the Apostolic office or Permanent secretariats as the case may be. Such distributions should be in terms of running costs only.

ii) Tithes (10% of all believer's income)

We have explained elsewhere that all God's tithes in the bible is for fellowship (sharing between believers). This is not money for a church leader to use privately. Contact our website and materials for more information.

iii) Seeds (gifts and giving served the church for carnal or earthly rewards)

Asking for seeds from Christians is strictly prohibited. The word of God says that freely we received and freely we must give. Do not teach anyone to give in order to receive a blessing. Children of God are fully blessed (Eph 1:3) However, any willing offering in this category to help solve specific issues is welcome.

iv) Partnerships (giving for reasons to perform special tasks)

Partnering for specific works and projects are designed to help the ministry to grow and carry out specific interventions. Such request are not supposed to become routine except for charity work. Partnering for specific and general costs should be done.

Deuteronomy 25:4 maintains that we should have the joy to let church leaders have access to the fallouts of their work in the lord's vineyard. This word is reiterated again by the teacher Paul in **1Tim 5:18**. Therefore, do everything to allow dedicated leaders free access to their allocated offering funds. As they wish, they should be free to use the money allocated to them by ministry department.

> *1Tim 5:18 For the scripture saith, Thou shalt not muzzle the ox that treadeth out the corn. And, The labourer is worthy of his reward. 5:19 Against an elder receive not an accusation, but before two or three witnesses.*

Money from general giving and partnerships should be committed to the LA who should budget and plan the general expenditures including rents etc. I say again, do not be anxious about anything. The lord who can raise children for Abraham from the very stones can do a lot more for you. Stop meditating on how to "comb money out of men's pockets". What you have now is enough for all that He wants you to do. Do not teach men to sow carnal things in order to receive carnal rewards in this earth. False teachers of the prosperity gospel are already tasting the wrath of God **2Thes 2:10- 11**, they Now falsely think that what they are doing is right.

10.4 STRIVE LAWFULLY

Finally, let everything be done in order. All churches that receive and practice these teachings, will be endowed with the revelation of perfection. Perfection is the greatest word for anyone that is born again **(Matt 5:48)**. Many churches have this problem that many servants of God walk disorderly. I want all Gods children to use this book to help them start afresh with authentic ministry.

I have heard some MoG saying things like "Anointing without money is annoyance". To them, this very high calling they received from God is merely a promotion for earthly enrichment. What an insult. By the anointing of God, I'm vexed in my spirit even as I write this. Why would a man expect to be rewarded by God after serving without following the rules?

> *2Tim 2:5 And if a man also strive for masteries, yet is he not crowned, except he strive lawfully.*

It is for this reason that the lord cautions you in Luke chapter 16:9 to seek friends from those that are of the mammon of unrighteousness. See that you do this unless you want to rot in hell. Your price was a lot bigger than theirs; you were supposed to inherit all things. You became cunning and dubious in your transactions. Theirs was to dwell in the dark places of the earth. They operated in the flesh and some of them did play by the rules (we learn more in another series).

Let all your giving and receiving be tied to the gospel. I see many MoG giving significant things to their church members. A lot of them are actually rewarding these members for some service or the other. They have done well but should remember that worldly actors do it even better. Governments and cooperate organizations reward their own loyal servants as well. You must watch this.

Let your giving bear in them the marks of the gospel of Jesus Christ. The one(s) that receive should not necessarily be deserving of anything. You may not find this teaching directly from your bibles. The spirit of the message of Jesus Christ has never changed. Your gospel has been adapted for your own profiting **(Phil 3:17-19)**. Only greed and wickedness has changed in many of you.

I pray that you receive these words from the Spirit of God. Let us operate in the Perfection organizational plan to restore order in our father's house. Do not let the lord say to you one day "depart from me you that practice lawlessness". Do not serve God with your own set of laws **(2Tim 2:5)**. Amen.

> *2Cor 6:1 We then, as workers together with him, beseech you also that ye receive not the grace of God in vain. 6:2 (For he saith, I have heard thee in a time accepted, and in the day of salvation have I succoured thee: behold, now is the accepted time; behold, now is the day of salvation.) 6:3 Giving no offence in any thing, that the ministry be not blamed: 6:4 But in all things approving ourselves as the ministers of God, in much patience, in afflictions, in necessities, in distresses, 6:5 In stripes, in imprisonments, in tumults, in labours, in watchings, in fastings; 6:6 By pureness, by knowledge, by longsuffering, by kindness, by the Holy Ghost, by love unfeigned, 6:7 By the word of truth, by the power of God, by the armour of*

The lord spares no one. Do not allow yourself be punched in the face by inactivity. The lord will require from you dividends for his word (talents) invested in you. Your ministry is supposed to cause many others to receive salvation with you. If you waste this word, you will regret eternally (Matt 25:14-28). You were saved with a huge price.

Consider most salary earners in Christian ministry. Their biological children never continue in their footsteps. Theirs was just a job for money and not a calling from God (except for those whose churches are family businesses). Put full worth into your ministry. Your ministry is not where you go to church, where you sing praises and worship. It goes beyond that. It is this work we do after hearing God.

This book is an opportunity to know thyself, even as you love to shout towards others at the top of your voice. You now know your ministry is fake. You have collected tithes and kept for yourself whereas the word says tithes belong to the sanctified **(Num 18:21)**. You have fed fat to the offerings whereas the word says you are as a muzzled ox working for a master who lives in the spirit. Listen. You are just a service ox. The master tells you what to do or not.

Some have seen and read these scriptures in the past without understanding. Yet many others have ignored them altogether. Are you happy after learning these truths? If you are happy then there is love inside of you. If somehow you are unhappy after learning this, then bye bye. Your destination is hell fire with your fellow haters of truth **(2Thes 2:12)**.

1Cor 13:6 Rejoiceth not in iniquity, but rejoiceth in the truth.

All falsehood is hereby banished from the church of Jesus Christ. Anyone that is called by the lord henceforth, must learn and work with entitlements, not titles.

Perfection ministry (**1Cor13:10**) by CMO recognizes only the entitled ministers of the gospel. All the rest are branded "fake". As a teacher I urge you to treat this issue with the utmost importance. We must make this change happen. All ministry offices according to **Ephesians 4:11** should be used for the edification of believers. Contact our ministry, help us spread the truth. Fake ministers have more money than they can spend, yet the truth has been ignored to the level that He (truth) has nowhere to lay His head even in the so called "houses of God". What a shame. They act God without listening to God. This is even as it should be **(Matt 8:20)**.

We cannot stop believers to receive their daily bread. You are free indeed to collect from others. The teacher Paul says this is not the ideal way of doing things. The essence of CMO is to help you see that Christian ministry is for you to groom others fully into the same gospel you received by following the entitled gifts of God. That they too may be instruments used of God for expanding his kingdom.

> *1Cor 9:12 If others be partakers of this power over you, are not we rather? Nevertheless, we have not used this power; but suffer all things, lest we should hinder the gospel of Christ. 9:13 Do ye not know that they which minister about holy things live of the things of the temple? and they which wait at the altar are partakers with the altar? 9:14 Even so hath the Lord ordained that they which preach the gospel should live of the gospel. 9:15 But I have used none of these things: neither have I written these things, that it should be so done unto me: for it were better for me to die, than that any man should make my glorying void. 9:16 For though I preach the gospel, I have nothing to glory of: for necessity is laid upon me; yea, woe is unto me, if I preach not the gospel! 9:17 For if I do this thing willingly, I have a reward: but if against my will, a dispensation of the gospel is committed unto me.*

We see from **1Cor 9:12-17** that the teacher Paul says these things not because dedicated ministers cannot make use of the contributions we make for the gospel. Rather, the problem is that without a good CMO, the phenomenon of prosperity derails many into perdition **(Luke 8:14)**. They become greedy and minding of worldly things. Even so, to live of the gospel **(1Cor 9:14)** is addressing your needs. Jesus did not say that God will provide your wants. He said the lord will provide all our needs **(Matt 6:32-35)**. Do not confuse wants and needs. Wants are limitless. Needs are few.

The prescribed norm therefore covers a running cost; being muzzled to the ministry. Not feeding fat from God's business. Structuring CMO is helping us to do this essential work.

We have preachers who spend all their time boasting on wealth. Having multiple riches and spending all of that in extravagance. Our lord was not like that. He asked that the crumbs of the five loaves and two fishes be collected. That NOTHING be wasted. Beware of evil workers. By their fruits you know them. How can Jesus be lord of someone who will travel miles in a private jet to go do make up? How? Are you so foolish to understand that these people are worldly?

Stop following people who do not follow Christ. They will not tell you that their hearts are evil. By their bad fruits you should know them. I tell you to wake up from this prosperity nonsense. We are not saying that Christians should not meet needs in the gospel. That is the reason God put in place the giving in the first place. I am a medical doctor. I can afford certain extras in life. But if I can do economically to save for a hungry stomach, I will always be glad to do just that.

The teacher Paul set the ideal model of the New Testament minister of the gospel. Do not abuse your power in the gospel of our lord **(1Cor 9:12)**. Be an example to all men. Take off ministry with a full inclination of service. The lord knows what you are up to.

> *Psalms 38:9 Lord, all my desire is before thee; and my groaning is not hid from thee.*

It is written, that man shall not live by bread alone **(Matt 4:4, Luke 4:4)** You do not start a church hoping fervently that one day it feeds you and your household. That is a private business. If you are like that, then you are either a goat or wolf in sheep's clothing. I advice you to repent before doom comes your way. Forget about anointing. Anointing **(Matt 7:23)** is of no purpose when God checks your work. The devil was also anointed even more than you. No matter how difficult things are for you now, remember that hell fire is a lot worse. Repent therefore.

CHAPTER 11: FOLLOWERS or SUPPORTERS

« Brainwashing in Ministry »

> *[[Preach the word; be instant in season, out of season; reprove, rebuke, exhort with all longsuffering and doctrine. 2Tim 4:2]]*

There is this saying about a leader,

A LEADER MAKES YOU

"DO THINGS YOU COULD NOT IMAGINE

A boss on the other hand "causes you to do even those things you would rather never want to do". This brings us to understand the concepts of followers and or supporters. The leader is that person who has followers but the boss can only have supporters.

These two bear different types of fruits. To cause someone to either support or follow, you have to communicate with them through a type of "BRAINWASH". They get to decide to follow you depending on two principles. The inclusion or exclusion principles. **Supporters are made through the « exclusion principle » while followers are made by inclusion**

11.1 MAKING SUPPORTERS

It is easier to make supporters than followers but much too easier to lose supporters than to lose followers. When you brainwash people by exclusion, all you do is tell them how that others out there are difficult, different and bad. They are not worth it, they are negligent, they don't have what "we" have, they perish, they burn and rot etc. That's it. Your supporters will be brainwashed. They avoid the strangers that they do not know. They can now say so many things about others even without ever meeting them. They trust you because they have a relationship with you to exclude others.

You thus support one another to survive even in perpetual deceit. If this support bond is broken, the empire crashes to the ground. Supporters then run to another boss and the cycle continues.

Supporters don't take responsibility for the message of the boss. There is someone always telling them what is right even without need of evidence. It thus becomes a thing of tradition. "How things are done around here". Supporters risk nothing. They can decline at anytime to belong with the boss. Jesus did not inspire people to support him. Even the biological brothers of Jesus doubted him and did not follow him **(John 7:5).**

No biology following. What transforms a man's life is not his birth. Rather a message that is received into the heart.

> *John 7:1 After these things Jesus walked in Galilee: for he would not walk in Jewry, because the Jews sought to kill him. 7:2 Now the Jews' feast of tabernacles was at hand. 7:3 His brethren therefore said unto him, Depart hence, and go into Judaea, that thy disciples also may see the works that thou doest. 7:4 For there is no man that doeth any thing in secret, and he himself seeketh to be known openly. If thou do these things, show thyself to the world. 7:5 For neither did his brethren believe in him. 7:6 Then Jesus said unto them, My time is not yet come: but your time is alway ready. 7:7 The world cannot hate you; but me it hateth, because I testify of it, that the works thereof are evil.*

11.2 MAKING FOLLOWERS

As for the brainwash of followers, it is a lot different. The leader and his followers are always in the same boat, doing the same business, having similar risks and benefits. The meaning of following someone is that you receive the same rewards or punishment. If they hated Jesus, they will hate his followers (John 7:7). Now is there anybody hating you? Your answer decides if Jesus is leading you. A minister of the gospel is not a member of a certain denomination. He/she is one that has a leader called Jesus Christ. His goal is to one day become like the lord. There are 91 no supporters in the lord's business. If what you are giving God is support, then it is not enough. God wants you to follow him. The bible calls us (sheep) children of God. We major as followers, not supporters of God.

Jesus talked about himself; who and what he represents in the plan and work of God. Brother Paul did the same mentioning that we follow him even as he follows Christ. In the same spirit, you have seen me say that I'm called a watcher over the house of God. I'm thus brainwashed and I'm brainwashing you by inclusion. To be included in the work of God as a partner. Do not feel jealous of anyone. Enter into the ministry with a willingness to build the family of God. Nothing else should matter.

> *LUKE 12:32 Fear not, little flock; for it is your Father's good pleasure to give you the kingdom*

You may find yourself in a church where you are instead being brainwashed for support. That is not enough. All you need to do is to connect yourself with the entitlement for the people in that church. The lord will use you to bring a spiritual change. Not pocket change. Even if you were a biological brother to the lord himself, what matters is that evil should be rebuked and righteousness exalted. Belonging is not passive; it is about choices and actions.

Many false denominations today have ordained or appointed people to "brainwash support". They remain in charge forever. You are in a church but have no opinion in changing the world. You hear the Holy Spirit speaking to you everyday about the wrong things in the world. Sometimes the ones you were supposed to look up to for spiritual solutions are worse off. Who do you think should make the difference? You of course.

Only a leader can cause others to become dedicated; by helping them to do followership. If you are not part of the team working hard for the lord, you are not a Christian. Denomination will lead nobody to the lord. If the person at the forefront is not using the word of God to cause you to live right and to become a leader yourself, you just have to leave the place. This is sanctification. The starting point which we studied at the beginning of this book. God uses only the sanctified.

When God brainwashes you, you too will brainwash others into the same kingdom. You feel good about doing it. You know all the details of his business. Unlike so many that have groomed mainly their biological families as leaders, you should not do this. The spiritual family is for everyone. It does not matter what they did or did not do. The call to minister appears to all men that are approved by God.

Unfortunately, many of you "Christians" are foolish supporters. A result of the failing Christian Ministry organization pattern of our day whose many leaders are wolves in sheep clothing. I pray that this book helps you become what God has planned for your own ministry (1Tim 1:12). If your name is Charles Watcher, there is no problem naming your ministry as « Charles Watcher Ministries International » for example. The more important thing is to inspire "followers". Secondly, the calling you received from God (perfection for example) is more important than your fame.

When men brainwash you, their objective is for private gain. To grow by supporters. They may not be growing spiritually so too your growth means nothing. You do not belong with them that enjoy the financial booty. You are fooled. As days pass, Followers grow in the spirit but supporters shrink. If you are truly maturing spiritually, it will be easy for you to connect with the vision of perfection (Matt 5:48) which is also for the end time (1Cor 13:10).

11.3 CALLING TYPE AND RESPONSIBILITY

For the purpose of our present work, we encourage all ministers to get dedicated being sanctified, separate yourself from all wrong doctrines and be used by the lord where you are;

Denominational believers: Commit the church to a Christian ministry using the word of God based on the works and power of the Holy Spirit.

Perfection Ministry entitled officers: Empower Christians with the elements of perfection as directed by the lord.

To follow Jesus is not to trail behind him in some physical march past. No. That's a symbol. To follow Jesus is to listen and to do all the teachings He gives us.

> *2Tim 2:6 The husbandman that laboureth must be first partaker of the fruits.*

11.4 LOVE IN OUR FELLOWSHIP

John 17:11 And now I am no more in the world, but these are in the world, and I come to thee. Holy Father, keep through thine own name those whom thou hast given me, that they may be one, as we are. 17:23 I in them, and thou in me, that they may be made perfect in one; and that the world may know that thou hast sent me, and hast loved them, as thou hast loved me.

True believers love themselves. Jesus prayed that we be one in **John 17:11**. You might have named your ministry "Enter Heaven at the Speed of light Embassy". The lord is not interested in that. The lord wants us to love all the believers. You must extend a hand of fellowship to other Christians. Not because you want them to be under your financial control. Not because you want them to serve in your particular ministry. No exploitation. Serve others in love.

No. Love them and help them because we all are one in the lord. **Filial love** is not negotiable. Your perfection is not complete **(John 17:23)** until you start doing fellowship with all believers. Not even the different or contrasting doctrines they seem to preach should stop you **(Heb 6:1-2)**.

All acts of perfection is birthed first of all as a call to sanctification with the lord **(Heb 2:11)** and heading towards a divine oneness **(John 17:23)**. This book is for your own good. No oneness no perfection. This word is for all pastors. Perfection makes us become like Jesus. You are your brother's keeper. Irresponsibility kills vision. Do not enter ministry until you are willing to take responsibility IN FULL. No place for excuses. Do not also waste time, keeping or grooming people who are experts at giving excuses. These are the hypocrites **(Luke 9:62)**. Anyone that will minister to the lord, runs towards truth. Truth does not force Himself on anybody.

If your ministry is for the lord, you should take-off without any plans for reward from men **(3John1:7)**. Otherwise do not come near me. My path is one of perfection. You must lay down your life for the brethren.

3John 1:7 Because that for his name's sake they went forth, TAKING NOTHING of the Gentiles.

The followers of perdition after Judas are in the churches teaching « the goats » and trying to deceive if it were possible even the very elect **(Matt 24:24)**. Notice that Jesus called Judas a devil.

John 6:70 Jesus answered them, Have not I chosen you twelve, and one of you is a devil?

Today's lovers of money are dangerous. Their hearts no longer care to receive or emit sound doctrine; choked by the cares of this world, the riches and prestige from the things of men **(Luke 8:14).** I remind you of the parables of the kingdom of God below. Understand scripture;

Both goats and sheep stayed together until the end (Matt 25:33), Both the good and bad fish were together until the selection after the fisherman went on land. Do not consider these people in your churches to be your mentors. Many of them are goats of wolves and bad fish to be discarded by the lord soon. They don't do the word of God.

They will collect even from the poorest and spend on lavished gifts to their friends and expensive hotel bills, houses and locomotives. I tell you, their own followers are become so callous with them that they do not realize the plight of the poor and needy. Yet in pretence they speak about heaven. Beware less you too fall into this folly.

Christian ministry is built in hearts and followers: not on tangible buildings and supporters. Mere support of any kind is an artificial concept in Christianity. Your money alone is not enough. If you are not a follower of Jesus Christ, do not support me. But if you follow me as I follow Christ, go ahead and start your own ministry... I will support you. The lord bless you. Amen.

11.5 BACKSLIDING

This is a term often used erroneously by believers to describe anyone that strays away from the faith. Ministers of the gospel shouldn't teach that backsliders are people who leave the faith by entering into sinful actions. Any act void of love is sin. Even the ones that have now turned God's business into their profitable organizations. These have turned away from the faith altogether.

> *Heb 6:4 For it is impossible for those who were once enlightened, and have tasted of the heavenly gift, and were made partakers of the Holy Ghost, 6:5 And have tasted the good word of God, and the powers of the world to come, 6:6 If they shall fall away, to renew them again unto repentance; seeing they crucify to themselves the Son of God afresh, and put him to an open shame.*

Beware of the false teachers in the world. A backslider is someone who stopped production or reduced his production capacity. When the youngr son took his father's money and went off to spend in a far-off land, he did nothing sinful (Luke 15:11-32). He wasted his father's money. The only problem was that he was not productive during that time. There are some people whose Christianity is coming to sit in a church once in a while. There is no follower of God that does not work for the kingdom. The ones that enter into sin and will not repent should be put away from amongst the believers (1Cor5:11).

We are ministers of the gospel called to work in all seasons. When a minister reduces preaching or teaching activities, such has backslidden.

> *Luke 9:62 ... No man, having put his hand to the plow, and looking back, is fit for the kingdom of God*

CHAPTER 12: Patience in the GOSPEL NET

[[Again, the kingdom of heaven is like unto a net, that was cast into the sea, and gathered of every kind: Matt 13:47]]

12.1 DO SOMETHING, GET ALL THINGS

Before talking Christianity, I will like to address the burden of religion. There is not a day Jesus promoted religion or went about insisting that religious ceremonies of his day should be carried out. He instead discouraged people from this kind of perception. The sole purpose to his mission was to work and teach Godly love which is righteousness.

> Inside this gospel net, there are always sheep vs goats or good vs bad fish or good fruits vs weeds. Their leaders also are many wolves vs few shepherds

Do not think that after attending or presiding over millions of "Christian ceremonies" often called mass in some cases, then you shall become more spiritually fulfilled. No. Fulfillment will come to you only as you start doing something to bring more love into your world. You must take a definite step. Do something about what is not going right around you.

The greatest enemy of Christianity is not unbelievers or atheists but religion. Religion makes you think that to serve God is to multiply ceremonies and sit together singing or sitting and standing or kneeling in any ritual obedience or tradition. Ceremonial robes, procedures of conduct etc become key. That is exactly why many people get hooked behind. They become expert displayers of a religious culture where little or no attention is given to the key things that work for love.

If you are in a religion, there is a very high chance you do not know the Holy Spirit. You cannot follow the Holy Spirit unless you are free as the wind (**John 3:8**), going where he wills. Religion makes sure that your attention is grounded in ceremonial rituals that have no use at all.

Did you ever hear that Jesus went to the synagogue and knelt, or bowed or stoned a wall or faced a direction etc etc? No. All we hear is that he spoke words to straighten love and fix the errors in men's lives. Even when he was to be baptized by water, he said it (this ceremony) was not necessary. (I got baptized with the Holy Spirit before being talked into water baptism). So why crowd around ceremonies?

The man that awaits the Holy Spirit, I tell you, does not queue around ceremonial stands. That man is looking inwards and straightening the wrongs in his heart; seeking no notice from men. **You should have nothing to do with religion**. You were called a minister by the lord to get his word to the nations. Not to be sitting around wasting time with men's ideas. You should identify religion easily.

12.2 HOW TO IDENTIFY RELIGION

i) A religion is a "gathering" that makes you loyal to "wordless" ceremonies. In religion, it is very important for them to ring a bell, light a candle or put up a statue or crucifix than to check which word from the spirit is appropriate at that time. If a wonderful alter or decoration is present, they feel extra accomplished. They praise these things than they are eager to talk about God. They sing to other things or idolize them because they do not want to test their faith regularly if they talk directly with God. Here is the question they cannot answer If the statue is not God, why not get rid of it altogether? No they think that the statue will help them somehow.

ii) It becomes a tradition in them to bow, kneel, stand, etc at particular times. It is often seen that they do not care that idolatry is a part of these routine practices which they forcefully attribute to God (Exod 20:4-5, Exod 20:25)

iii)It is highly institutionalized with protocol for titles of honour to prevail instead of entitlements for service.

iv)People feel happy and are brainwashed to think their actions will help them expand them spiritually whereas there is no word helping them to transform inside. You will see a lot of them sinning and attending ceremonies regularly.

v)Religions and their leaders are never conscious of the fact that there are sinners in the world and that they are called by the lord to stop the increase of unrighteousness. They cannot help themselves yet pretend to help others.

12.4 FISHERS OF MEN

The master's work is likened to going out into the world to collect men like fish.

> *Matt 4:19 And he saith unto them, Follow me, and I will make you fishers of men.*

Notice that there are three categories of events that happen during this fishing exercise. 99 We will study this from **Matt 13:47-49**.

ϖ The first case scenario is not to be caught at all by the net,

ϖ secondly to be caught as bad fish

ϖ Lastly to be caught as a good fish.

12.4 THE GOSPEL NET

1) First we have those fish that will never get caught by the word we preach. They remain floating in the seas of life void of any spiritually added value. These are the largest pool of human beings in the earth. These are the ungodly who refuse to listen to the message of the gospel.

They are not considered as part of the spiritual experience. God does not plan to judge these ones before they go to peril **(Psalms 1:5)**. They are condemned already **(John 3:18-19)**. To further understand this group, read up the story of the rich man and Lazarus of Luke chapter16. I have explained this further in my book "Dispensing the end time Gospel".

2) Secondly we have those fish that are caught but remain as bad fish in the nets of the gospel. They are also referred to as the goats **(Matt 25:33)**. These were brought to the same environment and the pastures as the sheep by the preaching

of grace **(Eph 2:8-9).** They are the large masses that are church goers in many churches. They accepted the invitation to the kingdom of God but did not do the word of God. Many here don't know their judgement is for condemnation.

3) Thirdly we have the good fish representing the good sheep or fruits. These are the ones that are keen to listen to the master's message and to do exactly what he requires.

> *Matt 13:47 Again, the kingdom of heaven is like unto a net, that was cast into the sea, and gathered of every kind: 13:48 Which, when it was full, they drew to shore, and sat down, and gathered the good into vessels, but cast the bad away. 13:49 So shall it be at the end of the world: the angels shall come forth, and sever the wicked from among the just*

Catching fish is like preaching. This is for outsiders. Every kind of person comes into the churches after hearing the good news. Inside the church, there is teaching. Teaching is a hard kind of gospel **(Heb 5:12)**. Teaching allows for transformation of all who came in by grace. Rebuke always comes after the sweet things **(Rom 2:4)**.

Unfortunately, many people that were selected by preaching of grace stay in churches untransformed by the word of rebuke. They hate this type of gospel. Often even pastors are not yielding to the message.

12.5 PARABLE OF THE SOWER

A lot of believers do not still understand this parable. We can further study the three groups with the very examples of behaviour that the lord described in the book of Mathew by the parable of the sower. There are different characters that have access to the word of God. While God is waiting for fruitfulness, some are busy with other routines. Today anyone that has anything to do with a Christian assembly is quickly labelled as a Christian. That is too hasty and so very wrong. The reality is that many of them are sitting in the gospel nets only to be rejected at the end. God says this very clearly for all to understand. In that net, there are those

12.5.1 That did not understand.

These are the many ones that no longer have need for sound doctrine. All they can do is move round for "anointing". These are also the many in the religions who are happy serving God by attending ceremonies. They do not seek to understand the word. They take no initiative to do the word by faith. The word is of no use to them. We see shortly that religion like weeds fight productivity of believers.

Matt 13:18 Hear ye therefore the parable of the sower. 13:19When any one heareth the word of the kingdom, and understandeth it not, then cometh the wicked one, and catcheth away that which was sown in his heart. This is he which received seed by the way side. 13:20But he that received the seed into stony places, the same is he that heareth the word, and anon with joy receiveth it; 13:21Yet hath he not root in himself, but dureth for a while: for when tribulation or persecution ariseth because of the word, by and by he is offended. 13:22He also that received seed among the thorns is he that heareth the word; and the care of this world, and the deceitfulness of riches, choke the word, and he becometh unfruitful. 13:23But he that received seed into the good ground is he that heareth the word, and understandeth it; which also beareth fruit, and bringeth forth, some an hundredfold, some sixty, some thirty. 13:24Another parable put he forth unto them, saying, The kingdom of heaven is likened unto a man which sowed good seed in his field: 13:25But while men slept, his enemy came and sowed tares among the wheat, and went his way. 13:26But when the blade was sprung up, and brought forth fruit, then appeared the tares also. 13:27So the servants of the householder came and said unto him, Sir, didst not thou sow good seed in thy field? from whence then hath it tares? 13:28He said unto them, An enemy hath done this. The servants said unto him, Wilt thou then that we go and gather them up? 13:29But he said, Nay; lest while ye gather up the tares, ye root up also the wheat with them. 13:30 Let both grow together until the harvest: and in the time of harvest I will say to the reapers, Gather ye together first the tares, and bind them in bundles to burn them: but gather the wheat into my barn.

12.5.2 Stony Christians:

These ones understand and like the things of God but also love to be admired by men. They do not want to be stigmatized or named as disciples. They are ashamed of the lord and his words. The lord plans to be ashamed of them in heaven.

12.5.3 Christians of thorns:

I personally pity this group the most. These are pastors and "men of God". They heard and understood the word. Today they have had to distort the word of God in order to make money for themselves. It is a sad thing that these are being followed; especially the ones of group (i). The most in this group come from group (i). They were formally just goats but are become wolves. They have caused many to stumble into greed **(Mal2:8)**.

12.5.4 Seed on good soil:

Finally, there is someone that gets the right answers and receives on good soil. Good soil signifies that which is prepared to do the word. When you receive on good soil that is not the end of the matter. You have just succeeded to enter the kingdom of heaven by avoiding to sin. Receiving the message of God means you are a sheep (opposite of goats).

12.6 AFTER RECEIVING ON GOOD SOIL

The greater reason Jesus came was to give you abundance of life. This happens when you BEGIN to sow what you received. This is how you get total success. Emitting the message effectively, makes you a shepherd (opposite of wolf). There is a point in your life when this happens.

To succeed with God does not mean that all things are exciting outside **(Matt13:24-30)**. The ones that finally succeed to start bearing fruit are not free of problems. The enemy comes and sows stumbling blocks into their fruitfulness. Do not think that the trouble you have in your ministry is normal. No it is because you decided to bear perfect fruit. The enemy decided to make things difficult for you.

> *Matt 13:38 The field is the world; the good seed are the children of the kingdom; but the tares are the children of the wicked one;*

You will be surrounded by all forms of persecution and tribulation. There are always weeds in your ministry. There are also goats in your ministry. Like everyone else, they are also singing and praying hard. Yet they are from the devil **(Matt13:38)**. They cajole you with their sweet prosperity gospel, yet they are completely evil **(Matt7:22-23)**. That is why they never change their cunning tactics. They are all impatient. Here we discuss the lesson of perfection.

12.7 NO PERFECTION WITHOUT PATIENCE

Before receiving patience, you must be tried **(James 1:3)**. No fruit of perfection comes without patience. Those that are not patient enter into greed **Luke 8:14**. The minister of God must submit to the word of God **(2Tim2:5)** in order to play by the rules and not become hasty for breakthroughs.

12.7.1 THE FIVE SAYINGS ABOUT PATIENCE

I Our God is a God of patience:

(Rom15:5). Those who refuse to serve God according to the rules of his word are not patient. God is not in them.

> *Rom 15:4 For whatsoever things were written aforetime were written for our learning, that we through patience and comfort of the scriptures might have hope. 15:5 Now the God of patience and consolation grant you to be likeminded one toward another according to Christ Jesus*

II The testing of our faith is because we (like father Abraham) need patience.

We cannot bear perfect fruits without patience. A child of God should not build frustration after multiple disappointments. **James 1:3** Knowing this, that the trying of your faith worketh patience.

III Those who received the word among thorns are those that are impatient (Luke 8:14).

These are the many pastors that have turned the gospel of Christ into a profitable family business. They are now selling their worldly ideas of how to use the gospel to grow rich to other goats of their ministries. They are more interested in success than the rules of God's success **(2Tim2:5)**.

Impatient ministers are imposters who push down people during prayer to demonstrate fake anointing, they have a network to track information from people to use during prophecy. Contrary to the word, they teach sowing carnal seeds to get carnal rewards **(Matt6:34)**. They never talk about kingdom investment by giving the poor for example.

> *Luke 8:14 And that which fell among thorns are they, which, when they have heard, go forth, and are choked with cares and riches and pleasures of this life, and bring no fruit to perfection.*

IV To bear perfect fruits you must be patient like God.

> *Luke 8:15 But that on the good ground are they, which in an honest and good heart, having heard the word, keep it, and bring forth fruit with patience.*

V Perfection is the future:

Perfection is for all true believers **(Matt 5:48, Heb 6:1, 1Cor13:10)** and is brought about by patience. avoid hasty success in ministry. Your patience must first be tested. beware of the wolves

> *James 1:4 But let patience have her perfect work, that ye may be perfect and entire, wanting nothing.*

Productive ministers must pray to remain alert. Jesus tells us in Luke 18:1 to pray always. It is a lack of spiritual discernment that the evil succeeds to plant his weeds amongst us **(Matt 13:25)**. The teacher Paul instructs in **1Cor 5:11** to send away all that have the character of weeds or goats in our assemblies. The gospel of rebuke sends them away. No matter their physical contributions, you don't need a crowd of hypocrites or rebels. Perfection therefore urges believers to aim at perfection: resisting all elements of imperfection in the process. The more you purge others in your ministry, the less weeds that will reduce your own spiritual productivity. All our fruits are for perfection. Greed works against patience and fruitfulness.

> In all, the greatest problem of a fruitful or true minister are the tares (false ministers). Tares are the unfruitful children (of the devil) that minister alongside with us in the churches; yet their hearts are not transformed. We have all been caught up by the nets of preaching. Despite their endless complaints, be sensitive in teaching to minister to them always in rebukes. Nobody comes to God without a complete change of heart.

CHAPTER 13: stir up the gift

The prayer hour

Christians and particularly ministers should see the biblical viewpoint of Christian leadership that is not based on a worldly pursue of increase. The lord showed me a vision of the teacher and apostle Paul. I was yet a young adolescent in secondary school. I saw in this vision how he sat and wrote scripture alone in a small deserted room. Today I gladly say why this vision and why me.

13.1 MY MISSION

I'm sent by the lord to interpret these very words of the teacher Paul. These important teachings which many false teachers seeking gain, have perverted today. Listen to the message of the Spirit.

> *2Tim 1:5 When I call to remembrance the unfeigned faith that is in thee, which dwelt first in thy grandmother Lois, and thy mother Eunice; and I am persuaded that in thee also. 1:6 Wherefore I put thee in remembrance that thou stir up the gift of God, which is in thee by the putting on of my hands. 1:7 For God hath not given us the spirit of fear; but of power, and of love, and of a sound mind. 1:8 Be not thou therefore ashamed of the testimony of our Lord, nor of me his prisoner: but be thou partaker of the afflictions of the gospel according to the power of God;*

The gifts of God (**1Tim1:12**) are distributed according to his will (**Eph 4:11**) and purposes. You can have these gifts and never manifest them. Even as you get this word from me, these gifts are practically imparted into your spirits. The word of God says that you have to stir up these gifts. You have to activate the gifts of God inside of you for the benefit of others.

Let us always remember that it is God that has sent us. We depend on him to accompany us spiritually. God is spirit and not flesh. The word, the power, the vision all comes from him. To ensure that God is always around, we have to rely fully on his leadership. **How do we stir up the gift?** By prayer. Do not rely on your eloquence and common sense. The word says we should stir up these gifts.

I have written a book on the subject prayer "Textbook of the Christian prayer". If we pray according to the word, we'll be capable of maintaining and sustaining a strong dynamism of gifts. By the grace of God, I do fast regularly. I also pray effectively in tongues. That is why I am able to minister to you without ceasing in my calling to teach.

I pray for you that as you discover your gifts, the lord will help you to dominate and overcome all seeming and unseeming obstacles. That you may fulfill the full duties committed to you by the enabling of the Spirit of God. You will also face neglect, persecution, rejection and occasional lack of resources. That is no problem. Keep doing the right things. Keep praying and ministering to the lord.

> *Eph 3:20-21 Now unto him that is able to do exceeding abundantly above all that we ask or think, according to the power that worketh in us, Unto him be glory in the church by Christ Jesus throughout all ages, world without end. Amen*

Consider the example of Aquilla and Priscilla who started churches in their homes after they received the message of our lord. Invite others to your daily prayer meetings. Preach and teach without reservations.

> *1Cor16:19 The churches of Asia salute you. Aquila and Priscilla salute you much in the Lord, with the church that is in their house.*

13.2 PRAYER HOUR

Have a stable prayer hour like was the case in the word concerning the disciples.

> **Acts 3:1 Now Peter and John went up together into the temple at the hour of prayer, being the ninth hour.**

Praying effectively1 is a must for a minister. We carry along our temples (1Cor 3:16), and there is every reason to pray in it regularly. Challenge yourself to pray daily at the 9th hour (3PM). You can meet with other believers if possible. Read about the new sanctuary **(Hebrews chapter 8 and 9)**. Remember that the tabernacle of God is no longer in stone but with us wherever we go. As we pray without ceasing, our spirits will be stirred up in the gifts. Glory to God. Do not forget also to fast the Regularly Regular Fast (RRF).

Ministry is a call to follow Jesus. I have staked my life on Jesus. I only need the company of those that follow me likewise. The most painful thing that I've known so far is rejection. Jesus not only faced rejection with pain and grief **(Matt 23:37)**, he cautioned us to deal severely with rejection **(Matt 10:14-15)**. You will face painful rejections as well but do not give up.

> *Psalms 50:5 Gather my saints together unto me; those that have made a covenant with me by sacrifice.*

Do not reject my words. Any "believer" that rejects my words, rejects Jesus Christ. Stop all divisions. My words are not mine nor denominational. We continue with that which is set already

> *Prov 22:28-29 Remove not the ancient landmark, which thy fathers have set. Seest thou a man diligent in his business? he shall stand before kings; he shall not stand before mean men*

The lord bless and keep you The lord manifest himself in and through you I love you all in the lord, Amen. Welcome to the perfect day **(Prov4:18)** of Christian ministry organization **(1Cor13:10)**.

> 1 About prayer, when you pray less, you will know. If you sometimes feel ashamed to witness for the lord. You suddenly think you disgraced yourself. A praying minister never has shame for the work of God. If you are not preaching, you are not a disciple.

> 2 Remember love is the greatest **(1Cor 13:13)**. You would be called to love by concrete sacrificial actions. Our covenant to God is in sacrifice. Do not

trust in the gifts without love in patient sacrifice **(Psalms 50:5)**. Many have faith to move mountains yet they have not love. Love is patient and deals with rejections.

I woke up still working

In the morning of 17/12/2020

He was dictating and I was taking down notes.

It was a church environment

and many people were busy doing one thing or the other.

I took down so many notes.

When I woke up, I could remember three distinct things

he wanted me to do

1) to add CMF to the work on CMO

and to attribute that responsibility to the evangelists.

I remembered two reasond for the CMF

CMF Christian Ministry Fellowship

CMO Christian Ministry Organization

1) To bring together believers from interdenominational gatherings

2) To stop the abuse of the Holy Spirit

These are the things I remembered when I woke up.

Amen

APPENDICES

I) ABBREVIATIONS

BP Branch Pastor

CA Community Assistant

CC Crusades Coordinator

CMO Christian Ministry Organization

CRC Church Relations Coordinator

CSD Church Security Delegate

DA Deliverance Adviser

DTS Director of Technical Services

GFA General Finance Administrator

GN Gospel Net

GSO General Security Officer

HA Healing Adviser

HRO Human Relations Officer

LA Lead Apostle

LE Lead Evangelist

MC Missions Coordinator

MD Music Director

MFO Ministry Finance Officer

MO Muzzled ox

MoG Minister of Gospel/Man of God

PA Prophesy/Preaching Adviser

PBD Projects and Budget Director

PC Prophetic Council

PM Perfection Ministry

PO Prophetic Overseer

PS Permanent Secretary

RTS Redeemed Tithes Scheme

SC Secretary of Communication

SGVP Secretary of Gender Value Promotion

SM Supporter of Ministry

SP Secretary of prayer

SR Secretary of Resolutions

SY Secretary of YOUTH

TC Translations Coordinator

TDO Tithes and Distribution Officer

VB Vision Bearer

B) Colours of CMO

C stands for fruitfulness or productivity = GREEN

M stands for service and loyalty to God =RED

O stands for obedience and responsibility = BLUE

II) HERO'S PLAN

YOUR CONCLUDING PLAN This plan summarizes and challenges the reader to stay practical and focused.

KEY WORDS

Sanctifications, entitlement, apostles, prophets, pastor, teacher, PS, BP, LA,LE, PO, VB, Bishop, Deacons, Elders, ordination, dedication, ministry, organization, order, followership, running budget, tithes

What other key words can you add?

1) In which way(s) will you contribute to solve God's family crisis?

____

2) Identify your ministry entitlement. Pray and receive guidance from the Holy Spirit.

3) If you were to start your own ministry today, what key information fom this book will you use first?

Write them out.___________________ ____

Joseph is advising a group of Christians to stop going to their local church and come instead to his own. What are the important things to consider?

a) If he is right

b) If he is wrong

Hint: use Hebrews 6:1-2 and 1Cor13:10 to develop your points.

____

4) How and why will you set up a Christian assembly in your neighbourhood.

Hint; **1Tim1:12, Matt 28:19.**

Why is it important to remain connected to other Christians?

Hint: Explain the Christian tradition. ___________________________________

5) How many members do you need to be sure that God is working in your midst?
Hint **Matt 18:20**._________________________________ _________________________________

III) REVIEW OF WHAT YOU HAVE LEARNT
Introduction: Christian Sanctification

1) What is sanctification?

How will you know if a man is sanctified?

How are the sanctified related to the lord?

Chapter 1: Spiritual oneness

1) How will you agree or disagree that God's family has a crisis.

2) What are some causes?

3) How does CMO help to resolve this crisis?

Chapter 2: Components of Christian ministry Organization

1) What is an entitlement.

2) Name the five ministry entitlements.

Using the example of Jesus, say how each is related to another.

3) Why is it important to work in a particular entitlement?

Chapter 3: Christian Ministry Liabilities

1) How are ministry titles different from entitlements?

2) Select from the list below which terms in common use by churches are titles. Say why these terms are titles; apostles, pastors, priests, evangelist, deacon, bishop, archbishop, arch duke, arch knight,

3) Define the term minister and say how this term does not fit well with institutional religions.

Chapter 4: HeadBoys?

1) Why does the bible rank a conventional biship as more of a title than an entitlement?

Use the example of the ordination of biblical bishops to clarify this contradiction.
2) List the ordained ministry workers.

What are the functions of ordained ministry workers?

3) What is the difference between a pastoral bishop and an apostolic bishop?

Chapter 5: Christian ministry organizers.

1) What is the principal ministry entitlement of the teachers? Give examples from scripture.

2) What is the represented entitlement of the VB in CMO (after planting)?.

3) How many teachers are found in a church field at a particular time?

Chapter 6: Shepherds

1) What is the principal ministry entitlement of the pastor?

Give examples from scripture

b) Jesus made Peter a pastor (John 21:17) after he completed a good apostolic ministry. What does this mean to the perfecting dedicated minister?

2) How is the BP related to the VB in CMO?

3) How many appointed dedicated workers should minister in a particular local church.

4) Which are the appointed dedicated workers of the different ministry branches?

5) How are appointed ministers supposed to relate with a) BPs b) LA c) LE and d) PO.

Chapter 7: Administrators.

1) What is the principal ministry entitlement of the apostle? Give examples from scripture

2) In what ways does the apostle carry out this ministry entitlement.

3) What are the priority functions of the apostolic ministry?

Chapter 8: Preachers.

1) What is the principal ministry entitlement of the prophet? Give examples from scripture

2) In which core areas are the prophetic ministry leaders supposed to intervene?

3) Choose any three offices of this ministry and say what they do?

Chapter 9: Educators

1) What is the principal ministry entitlement of the evangelist? Give examples from scripture

2) Why is it important to interpret key revelations to the churches by the evangelists?

3) Choose any three offices of this ministry and say what they do?

Chapter 10: The muzzled ox

1) Does the word of God support paying salaries to its workers? Explain.

2) What is the difference between salary and running costs in CMO?

3) All the sanctified share of the tithes but only dedicated ministry workers partake of the offering. Explain the difference. Hint: You may need knowledge explained in the book "Holy Spirit's Money".

4) The muzzled ox is not worker is not working for itself but unto its master. In one sentence, how does this explain our ministry financial commitment on earth? General questions We have many private churches (businesses and religions in our world today.

Does God allow anybody to run a private church? Answer is No. Hint **Heb 6:1-2.**

Does God invite all Christians to run their private ministries? Answer is Yes **1Tim 1:12.**

1) From your current knowledge on CMO, what is (are) the difference (s) between
a) Private Christian churches and Christian ministry?

Hint: The anointing is not a sign that you are doing the right thing(s) Matt7:22.
b) Doing ministry and doing church?

Hint Observe the style of the teacher and apostle Paul.

2) What is the cost of preaching the gospel?

3) No genuine ministry can be received without understanding of CMO. Discuss.

4) Observe and comment on the CMO organigram below. Complete it downwards
by adding more actors for the different ministry groups.

What is the difference between a watcher(teacher) and a watchman(pastor)?

Use colours green, red and blue to define CMO.

SUPPORTER OR FOLLOWER

1) Can God's church function properly with a) Support b) Followership. Explain.

2) How is brainwashing followers better than supporters?

3) Backsliding in ministry has nothing to do with sin. How does this affect the
life of minister? Distinguish backsliding for the kingdom of God and the kingdom
of heaven (Hint: Find out the difference).

PATIENCE IN THE NET OF THE GOSPEL

1) What are the different categories of persons versus the net of the gospel.
Describe and give your best opinion about what they should do.

2) Sowing among thorns concerns the impatient minister. How will you help
others to become patient? List 5 things you will do.

3) Those that bear fruits are confronted by tares. How can this information help
the fruitful believer?

4) There is no perfection without patience. Write an essay (3 pages) on this topic.

5) What can you find inside the gospel net?

STIR UP THE GIFT

1) How, why, when and where will you stir up the gift?

2) How do you stir the gift up with followers?

EPILOGUE

I once travelled with a prophet friend, we moved round the city as I visited. While we moved, he was eager to prophesy to all my "HIGH PROFILE" friends. Of course his target was to improve on his local church attendance. I felt so embarrassed. He was doing things disorderly. CMO does not stand for disorder.

In the same way, many are "serving God" today only because they were jobless so they enrolled in a seminary. That is not the calling of God. When MoG receive salaries for example, a lot of them are provoked to a spiritual performance. They want to outperform others. When God speaks through one vessel, they quickly come in with something unrelated.

I have been consistently embarrassed with this disorder. **Ephesians 4:11** clearly tells us that God has called some apostles, some prophets, some evangelists and some pastors and teachers. Do not be uncomfortable with these appellations by the gifts. Understand the gifts of God which are entitled. Avoid disorderly worldly titles that yield no fruits. Neither be distracted by earthly riches which lead none unto perfection **(Luke 8:14)**.

The gifts of God are without repentance **(Rom 11:29)**. Envy not the gifts of others. If such gifts manifest, use them to receive more virtue from God. I therefore ask the church to be diligent and walk upright. The gift of a teacher has been made manifest to you through me. I give no apology to anyone that is resisting the Holy Spirit.

Treat yourself to entitlements. This book is a roadmap for anyone that is called into Christian Ministry. I pray that it helps us walk in order. Glory to God. Receiving Christian ministry is not about a physical building, it is a special calling. **(Matt 28:19, 1Tim 1:12)** The three pillar attributes of a competent Christian minister are;

FOLLOWERSHIP, PATIENCE & STIRRING UP OF THE GIFTS.

PILLARS OF MINISTRY

John 9:41 Jesus said unto them, If ye were blind, ye should have no sin: but now ye say, We see; therefore your sin remaineth.

It is excellent to serve the lord in ministry, but it is not open for anyone that doesn't have a ministry calling. For any man to venture into ministry, such a person must be sure of what he/she has inside, and that it is from the lord. This is because a minister is anyone that has said "I see". If a blind man says he can see, nobody will come to lead them out of their darkness. Be sure that you have light inside. It is better to say that you need help than to be a calamity to yourself and to others. Do not hide any wickedness. Be completely transformed inside **(Rom 12:1-3)**. Before seeking to grow in ministry, the first step is to assume therefore that you have said "I see" because Jesus the light is in your soul. Matt 6:23 But if thine eye be evil, thy whole body shall be full of darkness. If therefore the light that is in thee be darkness, how great is that darkness!

PILLAR OF FOLLOWERSHIP

The benefit of excellent followership enhances sanctification. The former baby Christian starts preaching (apostle, evangelist and prophet) and then later to teach (pastor). Remember we are sanctified in one with the lord **(Heb 2:11)** but many people are still far off from receiving the mind of Christ **(1Cor2:15)**. It is the growth of sanctification in one. How do you follow? The only thing to remember about how to follow is to esteem those that labour over you spiritually as very high **(1Thes 5:12-13, Phil2:3)**. There spirit of love is what enhances the strength of followership. Trust and follow those that labour over you except these ones are a bad example and need to be reported or rebuked or even removed from our midst (1Cor5:11). Followership has to do with discipline but shouldn't steal your spiritually "hard-earned freedom. In so many ministries today, followers cannot do good deeds because of excessive exigencies. They are not free because "businessmen" have kept them dormant for the lord. Everything is strict about money even if love is hurt. Do not serve God without connecting directly with the Holy Spirit **(John 3:8). John 8:36** If the Son therefore shall make you free, ye shall be free indeed.

PILLAR OF PATIENCE

The benefit of patience is that it helps to sustain a life of perfected productivity **(Luke 8:14-15)**. Ministers that are not patient quickly enter into greed. Their fruits become useless in the sight of God. Patience comes by a life of stretched faith **(James 1:3-4)**. How do we build patience? This is done by studying the word of the God. God is patient (Rom 15:4-5). Study in order to do service without greed. Many greedy ones bear fruits of imperfection and rejection **(Matt 7:22-23)**.

PILLAR OF "STIRRING UP OF THE GIFT"

Stirring up the gift benefits us by empowering and directing us to minister effectively and efficiently. To stir up the gift of God to manifest, we must understand the motive for this project of stirring up the gift as individuals. How do we stir up the gift? The gift of God that are hidden inside of you will only be revealed through continuous and fervent prayer. The bible says that praying in other tongues will edify us. Pray everyday during prayer hour **(Acts 3:1)** and other private time. Remember that the "you" here is your spirit. That is where fasting comes in. If you have to be healthy in your spirit **(Prov 25:28)**, then you have to fast the RRF. If your spirit is not in good state, your activities will be carnal most of the time.

ORGANIGRAM & COMPOSITION OF THE ENTITLED CHRISTIAN MINISTRY.

Heb 5:12-14 For when for the time ye ought to be teachers, ye have need that one teach you again which be the first principles of the oracles of God; and are become such as have need of milk, and not of strong meat. For every one that useth milk is unskilful in the word of righteousness: for he is a babe. But strong meat belongeth to them that are of full age, even those who by reason of use have their senses exercised to discern both good and evil

Dr. CHARLES PK, Watcher Vision bearer*** (Perfection Ministry)

1Cor 13:10 But when that which is perfect is come, then that which is in part shall be done away.

Perfection ministry is the only Christian ministry (non-denominational) on earth produced directly from the word of God. See that you honour the word of God (1Cor 13:10).